Two Weeks

By

Rebecca Patrick-Howard

For Lori,

Because, well, she knows...

Website

Want to read about more true hauntings and things that go bump in the night? Visit Rebecca's website at www.rebeccaphoward.net. Want to be the first to hear about new books or even receive them for FREE? Make sure to sign up for her VIP mailing list! (Seriously, she gives out hundreds of free books and prizes every year and promises not to spam you.)

Table of Contents

Special Thanks 2

Introduction 3

Laura's House 5

Laura's Stay 17

Hello Again 28

Laura's Story 33

Day 1 53

Day 2 55

Day 3 60

Day 4 67

Day 5 72

Day 6 85

Day 7 99

Back with Laura 106

Now 108

Why? 114

Author's Note 118

Visit Amazon 120

About the author: 121

Other Books 122

Windwood Farm *excerpt* 124

Disclaimer

Some names and locations have been changed throughout the course of the book.

Special Thanks

I'd like to take a moment and thank several people for helping out with this project. First, I'd like to thank my mother. She was a wealth of information where this story is concerned. I picked her brain several times over many years as we tried to piece the events together and keep them fresh in our memories.

I'd also like to thank my husband who has patiently listened to me go over the details of this account many times. He even humored me and drove me out to the house a time or two so that I could get the physical aspects of its architectural style correct. (I was young when I last saw it; I wanted to know if it still looked as I remembered it.)

Lastly, I'd like to thank the following people who helped me with research on the house and surrounding area: Theresha Capri, Bobby Barnes, Donna Cole, Bobbie Sue Hall, Lori Buckland, and Ashley Kirk.

Introduction

Although parts of it are going to sound unbelievable, the following story is true. The events occurred in the early 1990's in a small town in Eastern Kentucky. Although I was there at the time of the events, they did not happen to my family; rather, they occurred to a family I was well acquainted with. I vividly remember them moving into the house and can recall certain details of it, including the cellar and kitchen, clearly. In fact, I often find myself there in dreams. My part in the story is a small one. I was merely a bystander. However, I heard about the events as they transpired as well as many times afterwards. When people ask me what I think is the the scariest thing that's ever happened to me, I usually share this tale because even though I didn't personally live in the house, it left a huge impact on me. I recently met with "Laura" for lunch and she jokingly said I remember the specifics better than she does.

Many details have been changed, including the names of the family members as well as the name of the actual town. There are some privacy issues involved with this story and that will probably become clearer as the narrative progresses. I actually felt a little funny bringing certain events up to the family in order to write this book because I am sure some of them would rather forget they happened. In addition, the current homeowner would probably not welcome any publicity that inquisitive minds might present. This is a pity, actually, because if ever there was a house that needed a good investigation this would be the one.

Although the book is entitled *Two Weeks* and is predominantly about one family's involvement with the house, they were not the *only* family entangled in its malevolent web. I've now gotten to know *another* family who also lived there and had a similar experience, although I unfortunately do not have as many details about their account.

At the end of the book I've attempted to offer some interesting information I've gathered about the area through research. I have no idea if the area's history has any relevance on the events that transpired in the house, but it's probably as possible as anything else. I believe in energy (both negative and positive) and the area is certainly old enough to carry both. I think it's highly likely that the history *has* had an effect on the land and consequently the buildings that have been constructed there. If the story about the house's former use is also true then that would offer another plausible explanation for it as well.

It does appear that once both families moved from the location their troubles ended so I have no doubt that the house itself was haunted and not the families. As far as other tenants and why they weren't affected as strongly, one can only speculate. I would personally consider them lucky.

Laura's House

I had to admit it: I was jealous of Laura's new house.

Moving was not something Laura's family was unfamiliar with. In the short time I'd been good friends with her, a little over a year, they'd already moved twice. She and her four sisters and brother were pros at packing their belongings, loading them up in a U-Haul, and settling into a new place. In fact, they did it so quickly and fluidly that it had almost become second nature to them. Despite the fact that Laura was only eleven, she knew her way around boxes and could pack and stack better than most adults.

What set *this* particular move apart was the house they were moving into. "This is the best house ever," Laura had gushed when she first told me about it. "You're going to love it! I am soooo excited!"

I was jealous. We were moving that summer as well, but we were moving to an apartment in the middle of town. It was dark and cramped, smelled like stale cheese, and I couldn't have any pets there which meant I had to give up both my dog and my kitten. "Can't we just sneak it in?" I'd begged my mother. She hadn't been swayed.

Laura's new house was on five acres, had four bedrooms, and boasted the best climbing tree I'd ever seen. The tree was tall and thick with branches low enough to the ground so that one could easily swing up onto them and work their way to the top. "I'm going to build me a treehouse up there," her little brother Bobby had boasted, pointing to the very top. "And no girls will be allowed. *Ever*!" This statement had caused Candy, the youngest, to burst into tears.

Sure, it was an old farm house that probably hadn't been updated since it was built and was a little rough around the edges, but Laura and I could see past the chipped paint, creaky stairs, and mold and mildew that grew on some parts of the ceiling. "We can paint and fix all that stuff," Laura had said causally. "The landlord said we could do anything we wanted to—even paint our bedroom *green* if we wanted!"

It was the biggest house Laura had ever lived in and the first time she'd be able to spread out her stuff and not be on top of one of her siblings. She couldn't wait to explore the old barn in the back, climb the tree, and decorate for the holidays. Like me, Laura had a love of history and the thought of living in something that was a part of the past excited her. It excited me *for* her.

Of course, the big red stain in the middle of the kitchen floor *was* an eyesore and it couldn't be easily overlooked. "A little bleach will take that right out," her father, Jimmy, insisted when his wife pointed it out.

Jenny had grimaced, almost certainly recognizing that it was going to take a *lot* of bleach to get the house cleaned to her standards. She didn't complain, though. She was just as happy to be out in the country as her stepkids and husband.

Laura was my best friend. She and her sisters, all younger than us, spent more time at my house than they did just about anywhere else. As an only child I was envious of the fact that she had built-in playmates and I wanted her siblings for my own. When the girls spent the night with me, sometimes all at once, we stayed up all night watching comedies and horror movies, making baked potatoes in the microwave and piling them high with shredded cheese, and doing our makeup like movie stars. Their sleepovers were the highlight of my fifth-grade year.

Fifth grade had been rough for both of us and I was glad to see it gone. For the first time ever not all of our classmates were friends. Boys and girls were starting to pair off, to form "cliques," as my mother called them. Whereas in the past we had all played together on the playground and talked during lunch and breakfast, now some of the girls made fun of others' clothes and hairstyles. They broke off into small groups and pointed and whispered at the kids who didn't dress like them or live in nice houses like them. One constantly made fun of Laura's hair because she looked like Kimmie Gibbler on *Full House* and had a mullet. Another was always making fun of my overbite and the way I walked.

Without Laura I don't think I could've lasted that year out. I often found myself curled up on my bed, my pillow soaked in tears. We were kindred spirits, though, almost from the moment we met and had instantly formed a connection. Laura and I had banded together against some of the snobbier girls in our grade and effectively created our own little unit. We did everything together and could often be found in a corner, heads huddled, sharing secrets. People were envious of our friendship and even I, at a young age, knew what we had was special. Laura and I could spend hours together without saying a word, just content to be in one another's company. I couldn't have loved her more if she'd been my real sister and would have gleefully beaten up anyone who was mean to her. I wanted to protect her.

Now, however, we were going to be more than an hour away from each other. She was moving to a town so small it didn't even have a proper store and I was going to the college town of Richmond. We'd be at different schools. As someone who didn't make friends easily, I wasn't sure what I'd do without her and I consequently went through the first part of the summer dreading the day we'd leave. I clung to her like a burr, probably suffocating her with my neediness.

Despite my insecurities, Laura took my sensitive emotions in stride. She was a sweet, quiet, and thoughtful girl. What some people referred to as an "old soul," she came across as much older than her eleven years. Indeed, her sisters treated her like another mother. Her stepmother, Jenny, was only in her mid-twenties and looked like one of the girls herself.

Laura cooked, cleaned, babysat, and babied her siblings like a mother hen. She also made excellent grades, attended church where she sang in the choir, and was the favored student of most of her teachers. Her clothes were always clean and neat and she was nice to everyone she encountered at a time when some of the girls our age were really learning the art of cruelty.

Laura's father and stepmother were hardworking blue-collar people. Though jobs were scarce in our area and difficult to maintain for almost anyone, Jimmy never went long without employment and could do just about anything. Jenny had been the manager of several restaurants. They'd experienced a few setbacks but were persistent and tried hard. People liked and respected them. They expected their children to earn good grades, go to school regularly, and attend church. Everyone agreed that their children were just short of angels, in both looks and attitudes. I tried to emulate Laura's gentle ways, sweetness, and positive attitude but I often failed. I had a tendency to say the wrong things, act the wrong way, and irritate people. But I tried.

On the day Laura and her family moved into their new house, we stopped by for a visit. The girls were working like little beavers, even three-year-old Candy, as they carried boxes in and out of the U-Haul and up the steep flight of stairs to the second floor. Jenny was already hard at work in her cutoffs and tank top, her hair pulled up in a disheveled ponytail as she scrubbed at that scarlet stain on the kitchen linoleum ("tomato juice from canning," the owner had assured them).

Jimmy, meanwhile, worked up a sweat as he lifted the heavy furniture and carted it alone. They'd never hired movers—why waste the money when they could do it themselves? We'd never hired movers either. In our part of the state you mostly just relied on friends and family when you needed something like that done.

We brought along snacks and drinks for everyone and during a break sat out on the spacious front porch with the family. The porch spread from one end of the house to the other and they'd set up folding chairs so that everyone could enjoy the shade. The first thing Jimmy had done was hang the front porch swing, claiming that "every house had to have a swing" or else it wasn't "home."

Although there were houses on either side of them, they weren't very close. The countryside was wide and open, fields as far as you could see. Not a single car sped by on the road before us. The only sounds were that of the dog running around and barking and the crows complaining in the good climbing tree.

"Crows aren't supposed to be a good omen are they?" Jimmy asked.

Jenny shrugged and took a drink of her cola. "I don't know. My granny always said they meant death. Probably just an old wives tale, though."

Jimmy, not taking any chances, picked up a rock and threw it at the tree. The birds squawked in anger and went flying, scattering across the sky and leaving a dark stain against the blue.

"It's a nice place here," my mom ventured. "Very peaceful."

Jimmy nodded. "Pretty cheap, too. I guess they wanted someone in it before it fell apart on them."

"I like the house Daddy," Brenda, age eight, spoke up. "I think it's real pretty and my bedroom is huge!"

They were moving from a two-bedroom trailer so the amount of space was probably a literal breath of fresh air. Laura and her closest sister, ten-year-old Mary, would share a room while Brenda and Natalie, age five, shared another. Candy, the baby, would share with Bobby, the sole boy of the family. Two to a room was a lot different than stuffing everyone into the same one. I was jealous of the amount of space they had. Our new apartment was looking and feeling tinier by the minute.

Laura was already chattering about the posters she and Mary could hang on the wall, how they'd arrange their beds, and bickering about who would get the fan closest to them.

"Just put it between your beds," Jimmy suggested. "Then you both get the air."

Due to the house's age, it hadn't been updated with central heat and air. They'd placed floor fans all over the house, some in windows, some on the floor, and one even right inside the front door, backwards, to "draw the hot air out" as Jenny said. The air conditioning bit was the one area I didn't envy Laura. It was hot and stuffy inside the house, and just a little past June. It was bound to get worse.

"By the end of the summer you'll both be sleeping in your underwear anyway," Jenny laughed. "It's gonna get *hot* up there."

I jerked a little, wondering if she'd been reading my mind.

The house was built sometime in the 1920s, nobody was sure of the exact date. It was a wide house, with a large living room taking up the whole front. The only other rooms downstairs were a small kitchen and slightly bigger dining room. The winding staircase was in the corner of the living room and opened up to a large landing. All four bedrooms were on the second floor, along with the house's only bathroom. All the walls were covered in wallpaper, what had one time been new and fancy but was now faded, stained, and peeling. The kitchen, especially, was a bit of a mess with grease stains darkening the yellow floral print above the stove and sink. Laura, her sisters, and I saw past that and fancied it a mini mansion with them living like princesses in the country. "I feel like a princess," Natalie babbled. "It's like living in a castle!"

I had to agree. I wanted to live there, too.

The white paint on the exterior was chipping, the yard littered with paint shavings, and the porch sagged a little in the center. The handmade porch swing was a hit, however, and Brenda and Natalie rocked back and forth together, keeping time with their feet. It was pretty much a perfect afternoon and through my envy I was happy for the family to be in such a nice place.

It had been peaceful resting there on the porch together, munching on sandwiches and potato chips and trying to capture the slow intermittent breeze. I felt like if I closed my eyes I might even be able to doze. Suddenly, however, the serenity was broken by Lulu's feverish barking. Lulu, a normally shy and timid Golden Retriever, was going berserk at the side of the house. Her wild and frantic barking, mixed in with terrible screeches like she might be suffering in pain, had us all jumping.

"What the hell is she going on about for?" Jimmy asked, leaping off the porch in a single bound. He'd removed his shirt in the heat yet sweat was still pooling along the waistband of his jeans, leaving big dark spots. His brown hair was lightened a little from the sun and hung down past his shoulders in the back. The natural curls in it bounced as he started around the side of the house.

Curious as well, the rest of us stood and followed him, Candy toddling behind with a bag of chips in her chubby, dirty hands. "Doggy bark? Doggy cry?" she asked.

Laura stopped and scooped her up in her arms, resting her on her hip. "Doggy okay sweat pea," she said. "We're just gonna go check."

Jenny ran to catch up with her husband, her tiny frame looking fragile next to his 6'3" height and thick chest. "I'm gonna kill that dog if he's dug up my flowers," she seethed. Jenny had a thing about her flowers. No matter where they lived she had to beautify it. She'd planted the marigolds there before they'd even moved in.

Lulu was at the side of the house, frantically pawing at the dirt under the kitchen window, a good ten feet from the precious flowers. Jenny stood back and crossed her arms, satisfied she wouldn't have to make a scene. Lulu had already dug up an impressive amount of soil but continued scraping at the side, growling and barking as she worked.

"What's she doing?" Natalie asked. Her curly blond hair fell nearly to her waist, almost drowning out her tiny frame. Natalie was a beautiful, elfin-looking child. People on the street and in stores would regularly stop and take a second look at her, enchanted.

Laura shook her head. "I don't know. Lulu? *Lulu!*"

Ignoring her, the dog continued.

We all watched, kind of fascinated, as she dug and burrowed deep into the ground, spawning a large pile of sod behind her. I figured she might be after a mole or rabbit. Hopefully not a snake. Captivated by her obsession, nobody said a word and hung back a little, trying not to get dirt flung on them. Then, abruptly, Jimmy stepped forward.

"Ha ha," he laughed. "She found a window. Look!"

With one hand he grabbed Lulu by the collar and pulled her away. She grunted a little and then whined to go back to her job, but he gave her a slight push toward the gravel road and she sulked away, dusty and tired.

Jimmy was right about the window she'd uncovered. Sticking up about ten inches from the ground was a small, rectangular piece of glass. It had been covered by soil before Lulu's digging; none of us had noticed it earlier on our walk out to the barn.

"What is it?" Brenda asked, drawing closer. Laura hung back a little, still holding onto Candy. She stood with her hip jutted out in an awkward angle, balancing the toddler and taking the pressure off her legs at the same time. Laura wasn't a very tall girl; Candy was almost as big as she was.

Jimmy got down on his hands and knees and scraped away the grime with his fingernail. Using his hands to shield the glass from the glare of the sun, he peered in. "Huh," he grunted. "It's a basement. Or a cellar, more like it. Has a dirt floor."

"Let me see, let me see," Brenda cried, rushing forward. Bobby reached out his hand and knocked her to the ground, leaving her dazed. "What did you do that for?"

Ignoring her, he bent down and peered inside. "It's just a dirty basement," Bobby snorted and stomped away.

Brenda rose to her feet, dusted off her bright red shorts, and marched over. She squatted down and put her hands on either side of her eyes to shield them. After studying the room for a moment she stood back up. "It's got a big table inside," she reported to the rest of us. "Like it's nailed to the ground or something. It's really dark in there and you can't see much."

When I had my turn I pressed my nose to the glass, mindful of cobwebs. The room inside was stuffy looking, with dusty shelves, old cans of paint, and rusty nails scattered everywhere. With no light, other than what was coming through the window I was currently blocking, it was hard to see much, but the long table in the middle took up half the room. Brenda was right, it did seem to be nailed to the ground. I imagined it to be a work table or something for tools; it was pretty ordinary looking.

As I let my eyes scan the room, however, a dark smell rose from the dirt floors and began drifting through the window. It was a foul, putrid odor that accosted my nostrils and throat and sent me backwards, gagging and sputtering for fresh air.

"Ew, what *is* that?" Natalie cried, pinching her nose.

"I hope it's not the septic system," Jenny moaned.

Jimmy, who stood close to the house, coughed loudly. When I looked up at him, I could see his eyes were red and watery. "I don't know," he said, "but maybe it was covered for a reason. Let's put the dirt back over that sucker."

The girls and I spent the next few minutes tossing the dirt back to where it came from, holding our noses and keeping our mouths clamped shut while we worked. Laura stood back, stroking Candy's hair and murmuring something to her. She wouldn't come near the house.

Laura's Stay

Despite the fact that Laura had yet to spend a night in the house, and they'd just moved in, she wanted to come home with me.

"I don't care," Jimmy said, satisfied that the truck had been unloaded and they could get it back in time. "As long as she gets her bedroom set up first. Hell, she's worked so hard I'll let her go for a week!"

Excited at the prospect of having Laura to myself for an entire week I rushed upstairs with her, eager to help her unpack. It didn't take long to have her bed made, her stuffed animals lined up on her shelves, her books arranged, and her clothes in her old, beat-up chest of drawers.

Although I was a little surprised that Laura was so ready to leave her new house, I figured she needed a break. She needed a break from her sisters as much as I needed a break from my loneliness.

It could have been the heat as well. Even though she and Mary had the fan going, their bedroom was hotter than blazes.

When we got back downstairs, Laura's clothes stuffed into a brown paper grocery bag, we found Jenny cursing in the kitchen. "Shit fire," she hollered.

We walked into the tiny, stuffy room with Jimmy and my mom to see what the commotion was about and found Jenny staring at the floor, hands on hips.

"What's the matter," Jimmy asked, looking around in confusion. Everything *looked* ordinary enough.

"Look!" she screeched, pointing at the floor. "Just look at that damn thing!"

We all looked down and could immediately see what had upset her.

Although I had personally seen her scrubbing the floor with bleach for nearly an hour, and had watched the tomato juice stain completely disappear, it was back now, as scarlet as before. If anything, the puddle had intensified in color, its edges reaching out to all of us who encircled it. Jenny shook her head in scorn, lips pursed. Jimmy merely laughed and patted her on the shoulder. "Well, maybe you need to use something else. Lemon juice?"

As Laura and I said our goodbyes and started for the door I couldn't help but think that it looked less like a tomato juice stain and more like a pool of blood.

Laura's weeklong stay was one of the best times I'd had in my life. With my mom working during the day, Laura and I were left to our own devices. We'd stay up late watching movies, listening to music, or playing with my Barbies. Then we'd fall asleep with the radio on, listening to George Strait and Dwight Yoakam–two men we swore we'd marry one day.

"How do you think 'Laura Strait' sounds?" she asked in all seriousness.

"I think it sounds great," I'd answer back. "How about Rebecca Yoakam?"

"Fabulous," she'd giggle and then we'd proceed to plan our weddings, mentally designing one another's maid-of-honor dresses.

We spent our days walking to the park, checking out books from the library, or swimming at the university pool. With my mom's employee pass we could get in for free. One of our favorite places to visit was a small used book store called the Paperback Exchange. Not only were the books priced cheap enough so that even two kids could buy a few, she'd also take our books in as trades and give us store credit. We stocked up on "The Babysitters' Club" and "Sweet Valley High," sometimes sitting down with our legs crossed and reading aloud to each other right there on the store's dusty floor.

If we had any money left over, we'd walk around the corner to the bakery where they made homemade donuts with thick chocolate frosting.

Laura had been at my house for nearly three days before she told me the real reason she'd wanted to come.

I was lying on the fake bearskin rug in my bedroom floor, flipping through an issue of *Seventeen* while she stretched out on my bed above me, staring at the ceiling.

"Hey, you wanna hear something weird?" she asked lightly.

"Sure," I replied without looking up. I was engrossed with gossip about Fred Savage, my latest crush.

"I think our house is haunted."

I put the magazine down then and straightened up. Laura continued gazing at the ceiling, focused on something only she could see. "Why? What for?"

"Do you believe in ghosts?"

"You know I do," I replied. We'd lived in a haunted house the year before. We'd only stayed four months because the incidents had escalated to the point where something was happening nearly every day. There'd been no rest, no peace, and no answers. I shuddered to think about it even now.

"Well, when me and Mary were carrying our mattress up the stairs something pushed me at the top," Laura said nervously. Her face was a little pale even now as she remembered. "I got up to the top of the stairs and stopped to take a rest. Mary was screaming at me to keep moving so I lifted it up again to take a step back. And then something *pushed* me. Gave me a big shove, like it was trying to throw me down the stairs."

"Oh my *God*," I cried. "What happened?"

"I fell into the mattress and knocked Mary backwards. If she hadn't grabbed onto the bannister she would've fallen. We lost the mattress and it went flying down the stairs." Laura winced and closed her eyes.

I tried to imagine Mary, pale blond hair and big blue eyes, holding onto the bannister, angry and shouting at Laura for letting go. And Laura, confused at the top, trying to gain her own balance.

"Are you sure nobody else was up there?" I asked.

"I thought it might have been my uncle Brian at first, playing a trick on me. But there was nobody there. A few seconds after it happened they all came back inside. Everyone was, you know, accounted for and all."

I leaned forward, wanting to know more. After all, ghost stories were a lot more exciting when they happened to someone else.

"Did anything else happen?" I asked.

Laura nodded. "Later, in my bedroom, I was in there by myself pushing boxes around. I heard these footsteps coming down the hall. They were real heavy, like someone with big boots on. They stopped at each door, like they were looking for someone, and then they'd move to the next. I figured it was Dad or Uncle Brian, you know?"

I nodded in encouragement.

"But then," Laura bit her lip, "then they got almost to mine and stopped. I stood up and called out *'hello'* but nobody answered. I figured maybe they were playing a trick on me, trying to scare me. So I stayed real quiet and tiptoed to the door. I could hear their breathing, really deep and kind of like an old man. You know, wheezing. I still thought it might be someone pretending to be a monster. When I got to the door I stopped. I could hear them on the other side and see their shadow against the wall across from me. Something about it..."

"Yeah?"

"Something about it wasn't right. It looked too big to be Dad or Uncle Brian. They're kind of skinny, you know? This shadow was tall. And fat. But I crouched low and put my hands out in front of me. Then I jumped out into the hallway and screamed AAARRRGGG!"

I jumped back, startled. She giggled a little.

"Sorry about that."

"What did they do?" I asked.

Laura shrugged. "There wasn't anyone there."

I hated taking Laura home. Usually talkative with Mom or singing along with the radio, she sat in the back seat with me and for the entire drive gazed out the window and frowned at the passing scenery.

On the day before she left we'd visited the campus of my mom's university. In the middle of the campus there was a statue of Daniel Boone, his copper foot pointing forward. Urban legend said that if you rubbed it and made a wish, that wish would come true.

I had placed my hand on it, closed my eyes, and rubbed vigorously while I whispered, "I wish to be a country music singer!"

When it was Laura's turn she had placed her hand on it, closed her eyes, and vowed, "I wish to move in with Rebecca."

I'd given her a hug and then put my hand back on it and made a second wish, just in case.

"You can come back any time you want to Laura," my mom promised as we pulled into the long gravel driveway.

Laura nodded and chewed on her lip. She looked uncertain.

Her sisters and brother came flying out the front door when they heard the car, big smiles on all their faces. One by one they surrounded her, some clinging to her, but although she patted each skinny little arm back and kissed tops of heads, her eyes were dull. She didn't smile and I thought she looked lost. There was nothing more I wanted than to grab her and throw her back inside the car.

Jenny was inside in the kitchen, scrubbing at the floor again. "It don't matter," Brenda whispered to us. "She's tried everything. The stain goes away and then comes right back."

Jimmy, normally up and working on something, was stretched out on the couch, a heating pad plugged into the wall and underneath him.

"You okay Daddy?" Laura asked, going to him and gently giving him a hug.

"I don't know," he replied, wincing in pain from her touch. "I was just walking around down here and BAM! A pain sliced through my back. So sharp I thought I'd broke it. It's been like this for two days now. Can't hardly get up off the couch."

"Have you been to the doctor?" my mom asked in concern.

"Hello no," Jenny called from the kitchen. "You can't force the man to see a doctor. He thinks it's going to go away on its own."

"Probably will," he grimaced. "Probably just strained something from the move. I ain't as young as I used to be."

But, then again, Jimmy was only thirty.

"Our car don't want to start neither," Natalie stated.

"What's the matter with it?" Mom asked.

"Don't know," Brenda shrugged. "It acts like it's gonna start but then it don't. Uncle Brian come out to look at it and said it was fine. Pushed it out there to the road to hook up to his trailer and take it to the shop and it started right up. Run fine. Brought it back to the driveway and it stopped."

"It will only start if it's on the road," Natalie agreed. "Won't run at all in the driveway. You pull it onto the gravel and it dies."

My mom and I looked at one another, at a loss.

I could see that Jenny had been busy in the living room. She'd decorated the walls with Home Interior prints of angels, butterflies, and light houses. A gold cross hung over the couch and the thick family Bible was open on the coffee table. Their furniture was old but it was clean. Laura walked around, taking note of it all, as though making sure everything was still there. She nodded her head in approval at several things and pursed her lips at others.

"That damn dog keeps digging up that window, too," Jenny said, coming into the living room to see us. "And every time she does it that stink fills the whole yard. I guess it's sewage leaking under the house or something. Might have to call the landlord."

It was growing dark now and the house didn't feel as inviting as it did in the daytime. It was hot, stale, and even the large living room felt cramped with all of us in there. Although they'd just moved from a lot smaller trailer, this bigger room was crowded and stifling. I looked around in shock then, suddenly realizing how different everyone looked.

Laura's family was an attractive one. The girls were as pretty as the child models you saw in the *Sears* catalogue, each one with blond hair, blue eyes, and petite frames. Jenny was an attractive young woman with red hair down to her waist and a svelte figure. Now, though, she looked sickly and gaunt. There were dark circles under her eyes and her hair was matted and stringy, like it hadn't been brushed in days.

The girls were pale and poorly looking, with big hollow eyes and sunken cheeks. They looked like they hadn't eaten in a very long time. Natalie's hair, normally the shining centerpiece of the group, had lost its gloss. Even Candy toddled awkwardly, her usually chubby cheeks smaller and lacking their usual bloom.

What had happened in the week we'd been gone? Laura was the only healthy looking one in the group. She stood out with her tan face, bouncy hair, and bright eyes.

I didn't feel right leaving her there. I would've asked Jimmy for her to come back with me and would've gladly brought anyone else who wanted to come, but I was afraid he'd say no. Mom was also quiet and frowned as she looked around. Our eyes met and she pursed her lips, as though she wanted to say something but couldn't.

As we got in the car and pulled away I looked up at Laura's bedroom window. There was a soft light inside, probably from the lamp on her nightstand. It was the only room illuminated in the otherwise dark house. I remembered then that the living room lights had been off while we were in there, the only light stemming from the kitchen in the back of the house.

Laura appeared then, moving aside the lace curtains to stare out at our car. She raised her hand in a silent wave and then let it fall limply to her side. She looked like a ghost.

Hello Again

That night alone at home without Laura was incredibly difficult.

My mom and I stayed in our tiny, gloomy apartment and kept to ourselves. She watched television while I read, neither one of us saying much. Laura had been a breath of fresh air for both of us, always laughing and chattering and offering to help with things around the house. Now it felt too quiet.

Mom and I had talked about Laura's house on the drive home, about how something had felt "off" in it.

"Did you feel something there?" she'd asked me. I knew my mother—she was fishing for information before she revealed her own thoughts.

"Maybe," I'd hedged, unsure of what I'd seen or felt but wanting her to share what she'd felt.

She didn't.

I cried when I went to bed, remembering Laura lying on the other end of my daybed, her sometimes smelly feet up in my face. Her pillow was still down there, plumped the way she left it. I held it next to me like a security blanket. I hadn't been able to make any friends yet in my new town and didn't have neighbors my age. For a whole week I'd felt like I had a sister. And now I was all alone. Feeling sorry for myself was pathetic, I kept telling myself, but it didn't matter. I couldn't help it.

Mom left for work the next day and I slept in. Even after I woke up around noon I didn't feel like doing anything else. Morose and bored, I moped around the apartment in my nightgown. Not even "Swans Crossing," my favorite television show, could cheer me up.

"You've *got* to find something to do," my mom said when she returned home that evening to find me sitting on the couch and staring at the TV. "She'll be back soon."

I sighed, miserable. I'd thought of a million things to tell her, if only she had a phone. A couple of times I'd even pretended she was still there, using the bathroom or down in the laundry room. I figured I might lose my mind by the time summer was over.

Mom was right. I needed a hobby.

We were just sitting down to dinner when our phone rang. Not many people called us so it was a surprise to get a call that late in the evening. We looked up at one another in surprise, neither one of us sure we should answer it.

"It might be your dad," Mom said at last. "Better get it."

I answered on the third ring and was shocked to hear Jimmy on the other end of the line. "Rebecca?" he shouted into the receiver. There were background noises on the line, like he was standing outside on a crowded street. I could barely hear him over the roar of traffic. "I was calling to see if you could come back to get Laura."

Shocked, I turned to my mom. "Mom? It's Jimmy. He wants us to come get Laura."

Concerned, Mom quickly walked over to me and stood by the phone. We put our heads together to listen. "Is everything okay?" I asked. I thought I could hear Laura beside him, whimpering, but I couldn't be sure.

"She's, uh, just having a hard time right now and I think she needs to be away," he said, although his vagueness told us very little. "Here, talk to her."

"Rebecca?" she sobbed into the phone. It was hard to understand her. I didn't think I'd ever heard Laura cry before. "Can your mom come get me?"

Mom nodded her head. She walked away from the phone and began slipping on her shoes and searching for the car keys.

"Yeah, we can come. You want us right now?"

"Y-yeah," Laura cried. "We're up at the gas station but I'll be at the house. Can you please hurry? Please!"

"What's wrong? Is everything okay?"

"I'll tell you later," Laura replied quickly. The line went dead.

Mom and I worried for the duration of the ride. Laura had sounded terrible and Jimmy didn't sound great himself. "What do you think happened?" I asked.

Mom pursed her lips. "I have some ideas but I'd rather not say."

"What is it?"

"You're too young to worry about such things," she said. "Let's just see what she says."

When we got to Laura's house it was ablaze with light, every room lit up like a Christmas tree. Mom and I both scrambled to exit the car but before we could make it to the porch Laura was soaring out the front door, her long hair flying behind her in the moonlight. She attacked my mother in a bear hug, clinging to her and sniffing. I awkwardly patted her on the back and tried to give her a hug. Seeing her upset made *me* upset and soon I was in tears as well.

"It's okay," Mom cooed. "You can come with us."

Jimmy hobbled out the door a few seconds later, bent forward and clutching his back. He looked like he'd aged ten years since the night before.

"Thank you all for this," he said. "She needs some time away."

"When do you want me to bring her home?" Mom asked.

He scrunched up his face and looked up at the night sky, as though searching for answers in the stars. Finally, he let out a big sigh. "I don't know. I'll call you in a couple of days and check on her. See how things are going."

I was shocked. They'd always given us a deadline to have Laura home by. This had *never* happened before.

Mom just nodded and didn't ask any questions. We didn't hang around to see the rest of the kids. Laura was already pulling us towards the car, moving as quickly as she could drag us.

It was only after we got on the interstate and zoomed towards Richmond that I realized she hadn't brought a single thing with her, just the clothes on her back.

Laura's Story

Laura was in one of my nightgowns and planted firmly on our couch in the safety of our living room with a cup of apple juice in her hand before she'd talk to us.

She'd been quiet on the ride over and barely said a word as I rummaged through my dresser drawers and found her something that would fit. I was slightly larger than her.

"You want to talk about it?" Mom prodded gently. "It's okay if you don't."

Laura trembled and inched closer to me. "You might not believe me," she whispered, looking down at her hands.

"Oh, I'm sure we will," Mom assured her. At this point, she was almost certain it was some*one* who had caused Laura some kind of harm.

I nodded my encouragement and patted her on the hand. "You can tell us."

To be honest, I was dying of curiosity. I wanted to know what happened not only because I was a little nosy at that age but because I wanted to help her as well. I didn't know how without knowing what was wrong.

Letting out a big sigh, Laura put her drink on the coffee table and then leaned back against the couch cushions.

"It started as soon as you all left," she began. "Mary and I were in our bedroom. We had the windows up because it was so hot. We were just sitting on the bed, talking, when both windows slammed shut so hard the glass broke on both of 'em. We jumped, you know, and screamed a little. Mary got up and walked toward the one by our dresser, real slow like, so that she didn't step on any glass. It was everywhere and made a real mess. When she got up to it, though, there was a face staring back. It was just there for a second and kind of blurry, like maybe it was out of focus. But we both saw it. It was there and then it wasn't."

Mom looked at Laura in confusion, not knowing quite where the story was going.

"We ran downstairs then to tell Daddy about the windows but he was laying on the couch. His back was arched and he was crying, moaning in pain. There was sweat pouring down his face and it was all red. 'They're killing me, they're killing me,' he yelled. Jenny stood over him, trying to wipe his face off with a wet washrag. She was crying." Laura's eyes teared up now as she remembered. "It was awful. He kept crying for 'them' to make it stop. He told me this morning that it was like being beaten with a hammer all over his body."

"Laura, who is 'them'?" Mom asked.

"The ghosts," Laura shrugged. "They were beating Daddy. Jenny said it's been happening for days. They're attacking him. All us kids sat around him and I held the Bible in my hands. She said she'd called our preacher out to bless the house while I was gone. He came with his Bible and walked around, praying over everything."

"Did he say anything about the house?" I asked.

Laura nodded. "He said it had some bad energy, like maybe something that wasn't good happened there. But he prayed a lot and the little kids said they felt better when he left. But then Daddy just got sicker. We didn't know what to do. We linked arms and prayed for him, prayed he'd stop hurting but he just kept screaming. Candy was scared and hid behind the chair and Brenda cried. The louder we prayed, the louder he screamed. Finally he stopped. He'd gone to sleep. Jenny told us to go upstairs, let him rest. Natalie helped us sweep up the glass in our bedroom."

Mom and I sat in stunned silence, both of us envisioning a group of young children, sitting around their sick father in the dark, offering childhood prayers above his wailing.

"Mary and I locked our bedroom door. It took us forever to fall asleep. We kept the lamp on so it wouldn't be dark. It was so dang hot, though," Laura said, shaking her head. "We moved the fan and plugged it in by our bed. We put it in the middle, between our beds, so it would blow in our faces. When I fell asleep it was there between us, almost close enough to touch. A little while later I felt something on my feet. It woke me up. I was kind of groggy, you know, so I wasn't sure what was going on at first. Then I looked down at my feet and saw the sheet was off me. The fan had blown it off. It was moved then, all the way at the foot of the bed. Moved probably six feet or more."

"Fans can move like that on hard floors," Mom explained. "Their vibrations maybe?"

"Yeah, that's what I thought too," Laura agreed. "I kind of liked it down there blowing on my feet cause they were pretty hot so I left it and went back to sleep. Then I woke up *again*."

Laura paused to take a sip of apple juice. Her color had returned a bit and she was looking better, although she still hugged the afghan she had around her tightly. "Mary woke me up screaming. She was sitting up in bed, kind of looking around the room with her eyes all big and terrified. Her sheet was off her, but it was all the way on the other side of the room, wadded up in a little ball. But now the fan was by *her* face. It had moved all the way around both beds and was blowing air right onto her head."

I tried to imagine a dancing fan, vibrating its way around the bedroom. The idea might have been funny if Laura hadn't looked so terrified talking about it.

"But still," Mom persisted. "It could have moved on its own. The floor slanted? The fan was unstable?"

"Maybe," Laura said. "Only it hadn't just moved, it was plugged into a brand new socket."

We sat there and let this news sink in, dumbfounded.

"We didn't sleep the rest of the night," Laura said. "We stayed up in bed together, talking about movies and trying to remember all the lines from 'Grease.' Daddy likes that movie, especially 'Grease Lighting.' He dances around and sings it. When he's feeling better." Laura's eyes teared up again at the thought of her dad, back at home, sick and in pain.

"Has anyone else seen anything?" Mom asked.

Laura nodded. "Yeah, we all have. When we heard others up Mary and I unlocked our door and went down. The whole family was trying to find Lulu. We could hear her, but we couldn't find her. She was barking up a storm and we looked everywhere outside we could. The little ones were running around, checking in the barn and shed, even looking under the couch. Candy kept saying she was somewhere in the house, even though we thought that wasn't possible. We'd checked all the rooms and closets."

Lulu was a big dog. It wasn't like she could've disappeared behind a chair.

"Jenny finally gave up. 'She's not outside,' she said. 'We've looked everywhere. That damn dog is just trying to trick us.' So we all quit looking and went back to the kitchen. Jenny had been making biscuits and gravy and bacon. I got out the dishes and was putting them on the table when Lulu started up again. Only, this time I thought Candy was right. She *did* sound like she was in the house. She sounded like she was right underneath us."

Laura's face grew a little pale again and I patted her, wanting her to go on and stop at the same time.

"Daddy got off the couch and came into the kitchen. We were all real quiet, listening. 'She's in the cellar,' Daddy finally said. 'How the hell did she get down there?' Sorry, but that's the word he used," Laura apologized. "We went outside and looked but the window was covered up in dirt. We haven't found another way to get in there. Daddy got down on his hands and knees, though, and poked at the floor. The linoleum was cracked in one big spot so he pulled at it. When he did, it came up and we all saw a door, like one of those trap door things."

I could envision it as she spoke, the dirty linoleum being peeled back, the kids crowding around the door and watching as Jimmy shimmied it loose with a butter knife and then tugging it open. Everyone peering down the old wooden steps to the darkness beyond. And then Lulu darting up the stairs and bounding into the kitchen, barking with joy at seeing her family.

"Daddy and Bobby went down there and looked around to see if they could find another door that Lulu could've gone in at. They were going to block it off or something. They didn't see one, though. By the time they'd come back up the whole kitchen was filled with that nasty smell. Everyone was gagging and Natalie puked right there in the floor. It was a mess." Laura shook her head.

She went on to describe how they'd closed the trap door and all the kids had stomped on the linoleum to make it lay flat again. Then they'd move a table leg on it so that it would stay closed, just in case.

"We were all too sick to our stomachs to eat so Jenny gave the food to the dog. She liked it. Daddy had some things for us to do out in the yard. He wanted to mow and wanted us girls to rake up the grass. Bobby was going to help Jenny with her flowers. So, we cleaned up the kitchen and then started to leave…"

Laura stopped talking then and looked down at the couch, her face reddening. My mom offered her something else to drink but she declined. We all sat together in the silence while Laura attempted to gather her thoughts, and maybe even her courage. When she finally continued, my mom and I were shaken.

The entire family had been together the whole time, nobody had been on their own since they'd gathered back in the kitchen. When they'd all filed into the kitchen to let Lulu out of the cellar the living room had been perfectly intact, nothing moved. Jenny and Laura both prided themselves on their cleanliness. Though they had few furnishings and like ours, what they had was older and worn, it was always in order. Laura herself polished the wooden pieces at least once a month and dusted nearly every day. There was no clutter, no disorder.

But now something had definitely changed.

Natalie was the first to notice it and when she did she squealed. Had the morning sunlight not filtered through the window in just the right way it might have gone unnoticed for some time. But with the way the rays of summer sun shone through and landed on the little gold cross right above the couch it illuminated it as though it were a spotlight. The gold sparkled, casting its own light across the couch and coffee table. It had never looked as radiant as it did at that moment.

And it was turned completely upside down.

The family stopped in their tracks after Natalie's initial shriek and stared at the cross in wonder. It was Jimmy who turned and looked for the handmade wooden cross that hung over the archway leading into the kitchen. When he coughed and sputtered, everyone else turned as well. It had also been turned 180 degrees and was now facing downwards. The archway was too high for the children to have bothered it; none of them could reach it. Jimmy knew *he* hadn't done it and Jenny swore it wasn't her.

Then who?

Jimmy quickly jumped into action and climbed onto the couch to fix the gold cross first. When he reached his hand out to touch it, however, he snatched it back in pain. Everyone had seen the sparks of static electricity that flew from the object as soon as he touched it. He stood on the cushions, gingerly nursing his tender hand and staring at the wall in confusion. "What the hell was that," he mumbled to himself.

When he attempted it a second time he wrapped a dishtowel from the kitchen around his hand. Even then, he winced in pain, both from the heat of the cross as well as from his aching back.

"It's like that thing is on fire," he said in wonderment. "Like touching a hot burner."

Next, he moved to the cross over the doorway. The girls moved aside, giving him room. When he jiggled it off the nail, however, it came loose too quickly and fell. Not wanting it to touch the floor, Jimmy caught it on his forearm and then shouted in agony. "Oh dear god, *dammit*," he swore, quickly moving it back to its rightful place. When Jenny moved to him and examined his arm where the cross had landed, she was shocked to see an angry red welt already swelling up from the skin.

"What's going on Jim?" she asked. "You turning into a vampire or something?"

"I ain't no vampire. *You* touch the damn thing. See if it happens to you."

Later, he apologized for snapping, blamed it on his back and how lousy the day was already going.

Laura'd spent the rest of the morning and early afternoon outside with her siblings. "None of us wanted to go back into the house much," she explained. "Daddy ended up not being able to mow the yard 'cause his back was bothering him so bad. Jenny made him another bed on the couch and he wanted TV."

Jenny brought lunch out to them and they'd had a picnic on the grass. "Y'all make a mess with them tater chips and boloney and I don't want to have to be cleaning up the kitchen again," she'd said when she brought the food out. "I'm still trying to get rid of that smell."

But Laura didn't think that was the reason Jenny was feeding them outside. "I think she was afraid of being in there too," Laura said. "She kept going in to check on Daddy but most of the time she stayed out there with us, working on her flowers and yard stuff. I think Daddy would've been with us too if his back hadn't been out like it was."

It was nearly five o'clock when they all trooped back in the house. The kids were streaked with dirt and grime and needed to wash up for dinner. The only bathroom in the house was upstairs. It was small and cramped with loose tile and antiquated features but the claw foot tub was big enough to hold two kids at once, sometimes three if they weren't squirming around.

Laura dunked the little ones in first, washing Candy and Natalie together and then letting Bobby have some privacy. She didn't want to get far from him while he bathed because, like a little mother hen, she was constantly worrying about something happening to him. Her bedroom was right across the hall, though, and just a few steps away. With her door open and the bathroom door open she could hear his splashing and singing. His flat little voice rose in volume as he went through his Alabama repertoire, starting with "Song of the South" and working his way through all the up-tempo tunes.

Laura smiled to herself as she made first her bed and then Mary's and picked up dirty clothes from the floor. She was also hot and sweaty but her bath would be last; it always was.

She was standing in the middle of the room, hands resting on little-girl hips, when her bedroom door slammed shut with a bang. The force of the blow knocked a picture of an angel off the wall and Laura squealed as shards of glass scattered around her. The picture didn't look like it had just cracked from the fall, it looked as though someone had stomped on it.

Shaken and disturbed, Laura warily eyed the door as she bent down and began using her bare hands to scoop up the shards of glass into a little pile. A bigger piece nicked her hand and when a thin sliver of blood appeared she put it to her mouth, tasting the bitterness and salt. She'd need a Band Aid and she needed to check on Bobby. She realized with a start that she hadn't heard him singing in at least a minute or two.

Still nursing her hand, Laura walked to the door. It was still shut to. The wind maybe? If a breeze had come through one of the other windows it was possible it had forced it closed. Bobby getting out of the tub and playing a trick on her? She didn't think so. She'd pretty much scared him out of standing up in the tub without her.

To Laura's dismay, when she turned the knob and pulled the door didn't budge. Hitting it with her uninjured hand she tried to unjam it. It didn't work.

"Bobby!" she cried through the door. "Bobby, are you okay?"

Nobody answered from the other side.

The keyhole was made for a skeleton key. She'd seen those in her grandma's old house. There weren't any in her house, though, at least not that she'd noticed. Could someone have really locked her in without her hearing it? She didn't think so. She would've heard them turning the key in the lock, walking away.

"Someone come let me out!" she called, beating on the door. "Hello!?"

Nobody came.

Frantic now, with visions of Bobby lying face down in the tub and his little face turning blue, Laura panicked. Using all her strength she threw herself against the door time and time again, crushing her shoulder and hip until they ached. "Let me out!" she cried, tears streaming. "Somebody let me out!"

In defeat, Laura slumped down to the floor, her head resting on the wall. Tired and scared, she wished her angel picture was still on the wall. The beautiful woman with the big, majestic wings following the little girl and boy on the bridge had always been comforting to her. She liked to think there was an angel following her around, protecting her like that.

When the knob turned and the door began to open, Laura scrambled to her feet.

"Hey, you okay?" It was Mary, looking confused. "What's with the yelling? You're about to give Jenny a heart attack."

Ignoring her, Laura darted past her sister and made a beeline to the bathroom. Bobby sat in the tub, the water now a dirty gray, and gazed quizzically up at her. He was playing with a boat and bucket and humming under his breath.

Laura's whole body relaxed in relief. At least he was okay. "Did you hear me crying, did you hear me yelling?" she asked as she helped him from the water.

"No," he shrugged. "But I wondered why you closed your door so hard."

With everyone else bathed and dressed Laura could finally have the bathroom to herself. She cleaned out the tub of toys, ran water for a minute to rinse out the dirt they'd all left behind, and then started filling it with warm water and bubbles. Everyone else had nearly used all the hot water already so her bath would be on the chilly side but she was used to that.

She knew she didn't have long because any minute Jenny would be calling her to come help with supper. With the water running she went back to her bedroom and gathered some clean clothes. She thought she was only gone for a few seconds but when she returned she was surprised to find the bathroom had filled with steam. It was coating the mirror and the toilet and sink felt wet to the touch from the condensation. Steam was rising from the tub in billowy waves. *Well,* she thought, *maybe the hot water situation here is better than I thought.*

    Standing in front of the mirror she wiped it down with a cloth, undressed, and laid her dirty clothes neatly in the hamper. Laura was just about to stick her foot in the tub when something caught her from the corner of her eye. A shadow, dark and fluid, passed quickly before the mirror. It happened so fast that Laura wasn't sure she'd really seen anything at all but when she looked down at her arms small goose pimples lined them, from her shoulder to her hand.

    Shivering, she lowered herself into the bath and quickly began to wash off, trying to ignore the crawling sensation on her scalp. She tried singing to herself, a George Strait song that always made her happy, and forget about everything that had happened that morning and afternoon. Old houses had personalities, that's what she'd always heard. Old houses made funny noises, had drafts, and sometimes smelled strange. She was just tired from the move, missing her friend, and not settled in yet.

    She felt, rather than saw, the thing that watched her. She didn't know how long it had been there, distracted she was by her own thoughts and actions. Something rustled in the doorway, however, and she stopped moving, her hands still entrenched in the shampoo in her hair.

The chills came again, quickly this time, and every hair on her body stood at attention. She was being studied, that much she was sure of, and it wasn't by anyone in her family. Forcing herself not to look at the door, the terrified Laura rinsed her hair with speed she didn't know she had and then pulled the plug on the drain. The eyes boring into her burned her skin, a cold heat that was shocking. She could see her heart beating through her chest, the skin moving up and down with impossible speed. Her blood was like an icy river, the fear threatening to freeze her in her tracks.

She needed to get out of the tub, she needed to grab her towel, but that would mean turning her head and looking at the door. The thought of what might be there stunned her in fear, the most vivid sensation she'd ever felt. "Daddy," she whimpered, praying he'd be able to hear her thoughts and come to her. She thought of calling out downstairs, bringing up one of her siblings, but her throat was tight. She didn't think she could holler if she tried.

With slow, easy movements she lifted herself from the tub and grabbed the towel on the back of the toilet. The softness felt good on her skin, its weight a shield against whatever was out there. Feeling stronger now she slowly turned to face the door, her eyes clenched shut and her teeth grinding against each other.

With determined resolution she gathered all the courage she'd ever had, thinking about the super heroes in movies she loved, and opened her eyes to what was waiting for her.

The figure that stood before her was just a few feet away. If they'd both stretched out their hands they could've touched one another. The long hair, dark dress that brushed the floor and delicate hands could only belong to a woman. Where her face should've been, however, there was nothing but a pale void.

"Ahhhhkkkkk!!!!" Laura screamed, her voice returning in a ferocious roar. "Dad-EE!"

The figure gave out a solitary hiss, like a balloon running out of air, and disappeared.

Laura was still standing wet in the middle of the bathroom floor when Jimmy and Jenny found her. Shaking and crying, they led her to her bedroom where Jenny petted on her and helped her dress. Jimmy marched up and down the hallway, checking closets, looking under beds, and making sure all the windows were locked.

There was no question about whether or not they believed Laura. They both knew now, for sure, that their new house was haunted.

"**Please** don't make me go back," Laura sniffed. "Please don't make me go back there."

"You can stay here as long as you want," Mom promised.

Laura nodded and moved closer to me. "Do you think I can come live with you?"

That idea thrilled me. It would be like having a real sister. I desperately wanted that to happen, for Laura to come and stay with us forever. We'd have so much fun together. I was aware of the fact that my attachment to her was probably over the top but we'd moved around a lot as well. I'd already attended four elementary schools myself and making friends wasn't easy for me. When I did make friends I clung tightly to them, probably too tightly, and suffocated them with my neediness. Laura, whom I'd first met through my mother when she was student teaching in her class, humored me.

"I think your parents would miss you," Mom said, "but you're welcome to stay here however long you need."

Laura understandably had a hard time going to sleep that night. We stayed up until the wee hours of the morning, talking and watching television together. We went through our repertoire of favorite movies: *Grease*, *The Breakfast Club*, and *Bye Bye Birdie*. When we tired of movies we baked a cake, using green food coloring in the batter. We were still up when the sun rose and conked out as Mom headed off to work. Having Laura's feet in my face again was comforting and I slept like a baby.

Four days went by without Laura hearing from her family. She worried about them constantly.

"Do you think Daddy's okay?" she asked one afternoon. We were walking up to the cinema on Main Street to watch Robin Hood: Prince of Thieves for the second time.

"I think they would've called you if he wasn't," I said, but I wasn't sure. It had been strangely quiet on her family's end and I was concerned as well. When we'd lived in our haunted house I remembered the sleepless nights, constant state of alertness, fear of what was going to happen next…It wasn't a nice way to live.

"Do you think things will get better?" she asked hopefully after we were settled into the rough, scratchy seats and nibbling on stale popcorn.

"Maybe so," I answered. "Maybe the ghosts just need to get it all out of their systems or something."

I did not think it would get better, though. I thought it would only get worse, as it did in our experience. And, even worse, I hope on some level that it would get worse for them—as long as it meant Laura could keep staying with us. I wasn't ready to give her up again.

Another four days passed by and then, on the ninth day, Jimmy called.

"You can bring Laura back home now," he said. "But don't bring her back to the farmhouse. We've moved to Winchester and don't live there anymore. I'll give you the new address."

Just like that, they'd picked up and moved. We'd lasted four months in our haunted house; they'd lasted fewer than three weeks.

"Maybe he just found something better," Mom suggested but we were unconvinced. We knew why they were moving; the house was just too much.

Taking Laura home was depressing for me but she was excited to see her family again, especially since it meant she wouldn't have to go back to the place she'd come from. The car ride back to her family was markedly different from the one where she'd left them behind. She chattered the whole way, talking about the start of school, how much she was looking forward to seeing her siblings, and how much fun she'd had at our house.

Their new house, a trailer, was much smaller than the farmhouse but larger than the last trailer they'd lived in. They had three bedrooms so the kids were able to spread out more, but being in a small trailer park it lacked the yard and good climbing tree.

Jenny and the girls had already unpacked everything and decorated by the time we arrived. They worked quickly. We were mostly surprised by Jimmy's appearance, however.

The last time we'd seen him his eyes were sunken in, his sallow expression almost ghostly, and he'd been hunched over in pain. Now he was standing at full height, his healthy tanned face beaming when Laura got out of the car.

"You look a lot better," Mom said upon seeing him. "How are you feeling?"

"Better now that we're out of that damned place."

We all went inside and got ourselves comfortable in the living room. Laura gave herself a tour of the place, stopping to hug on everyone along the way. Although I wanted her to stay with me, it was obvious how much she'd missed her family and an unjealous part of me was happy to see them reunited.

"So what happened?" Mom asked. "You all got out of there pretty quickly."

"You really want to know?" Jimmy asked. "It's a hell of a story."

Mom, Laura, and I all nodded. We were ready for it.

Day 1

Laura's sisters had not been happy when she took off.

It wasn't that they wanted her to stay there with them, they'd wanted to leave as well.

Scared and nervous, they'd all piled into one bedroom for the night, sleeping two to a twin bed. Natalie and Mary slept together while Brenda cuddled Candy. Bobby stayed in his parents' room. With little room to move, the stuffiness, and the events of the day stacking against them it was difficult to sleep. They all tossed and turned throughout the night, although the night as a whole passed by without incident.

When the kids woke up the next morning Jenny fixed breakfast and the day carried on as usual. Mary watched the younger ones while Jenny took Jimmy to the doctor. They stayed outside mostly, climbing the tree and running around. Nobody wanted to be indoors. When Brenda needed to use the restroom she'd walked behind the house and found a spot in the grass.

The doctor could only say that he thought Jimmy had sprained his back, probably from moving. He prescribed him some muscle relaxers and Jimmy popped two after picking them up from the pharmacy. Although they made him incredibly sleepy, they did little to ease his pain.

When Jimmy and Jenny returned home he laid back down on the couch and watched westerns the rest of the day. Jenny attempted to scrub the stain in the kitchen floor again and the kids cleaned their bedrooms. Life went on as normal. At suppertime they all ate Hamburger Helper and helped with the dishes.

Lulu ran around outside, barking happily, but nobody could get her to come in for bedtime. She refused to come any closer than the steps to the front porch.

"Come on, Lu," Bobby pleaded, tugging at her collar. "It's gonna rain tonight."

Lulu wouldn't budge, though, and held her ground. When Bobby climbed down the stairs and tried to wrap his arms around her waist to get her to go up on the porch she let out a low, threatening growl, something she'd never done before.

"Fine," he snapped. "Just stay out here and get wet for all I care."

The kids slept together again that night, feeling more protected in numbers. Worn out from playing all day, none of them had a hard time falling asleep.

Day 2

Everyone managed to get through the uneventful night in peace.

Nothing happened to disturb anyone and the older ones thought that maybe the bad stuff was over, that perhaps the house did just need to get it out of its system.

Jimmy thought about calling Laura to tell her she could come home but decided to wait another day. He still didn't feel well and it was summer break after all. He decided she might like spending more time with her friend.

Again, the day passed without incident. Cousins came over to visit and the kids all played together while the adults sat in chairs on the front porch, smoking, talking, and drinking Ale-8s. "I love Ale-8s," Brian declared, opening up another one. "Especially when you stink 'em in the freezer and they get that film of ice on top."

Everyone nodded in agreement. "You know that's why Jimmy won't move to Tennessee," Jenny said. "Because they don't sell 'em there."

"Hell yeah," Jimmy said weakly. He'd taken more of the medicine but he might as well have been eating Flintstone vitamins for all the help they were doing him. "Can't live without my drink."

"Hey, I was going to ask you guys, what's that awful smell from beside the house?" Brian asked. "It liked to have knocked me over when we got out of the car."

Jenny shrugged. "We don't know. We think it's coming from the cellar, though. It gets worse down there."

"A dead animal maybe?" This came from Sherry, Brian's wife and Jimmy's sister-in-law.

"You think you might have a sewer leak?" Brian asked. "Cause it smells like shit."

"Maybe," Jimmy answered. "I went down there and looked around the day Lulu got her ass stuck but I couldn't see anything. Haven't been able to walk much since then."

"You want me to go take a look?" Brian offered. "I can go poke around."

As a general contractor Brian had plenty of experience with these kinds of things and was good at his job. With permission from Jimmy he and Sherry gathered flashlights and headed for the cellar. The minute they peeled back the linoleum and opened the trap door the kitchen filled with the same awful, putrid smell. "Yeah, that's gotta be sewage," Brian attested, wrinkling his nose.

Sherry didn't flinch. "My scent's gone thanks to the cigarettes. This is one of those times I'm glad I took up smoking."

The long flight of stairs down to the bottom only prolonged the agony, as the stink grew stronger and stronger with their descent.

Soon, they found themselves standing at the bottom. Using their flashlights, they took a long look around.

The room itself wasn't very big, probably 10 X 20. The long table in the middle of the floor took up most of the space. Sherry walked up to it first and gazed down at it. The table was only about three feet wide, but it was at least ten feet long. At one end there was a hole. When she looked down at the floor under it she saw a drain, rusted orange with age and use.

"Hey honey, what do you think this was for?" she asked.

Brian, who was examining the pipes overhead and one big one that ran down the wall shrugged. "Don't know. Washing vegetables maybe. There's one of them big old farm sinks in here too. Probably came down here to wash 'em and maybe can, too."

One wall was indeed full of old Mason jars containing various fruits and vegetables that had all turned to vinegar over time.

Sherry didn't like the room at all. Although she couldn't smell the thing everyone else was going on about she was getting a bad feeling about the place. Sherry's mother had been one of those women who knew things before anyone else did. She said she could feel things coming to her, things she couldn't see or hear but *felt*. Sherry thought she might have inherited some of that, too.

Although the room was dank and chilly, as most basements with stone walls and dirt floors could be, the coldness felt like something else, inhuman. Despite the fact Sherry was wearing jeans and a long-sleeved shirt, the coldness found its way to her skin and clung to it, burrowing down into her bones and making them ache. There was nobody in the small room other than her and her husband but she felt like she was being watched. Not just being viewed, but being studied and monitored. The unseen eyes on her were probing, inquisitive. She walked around the floor, her arms folded tightly across her chest, her flashlight making pale patterns on the floor. Brian kept to himself, kneeling in some places, touching the wall and ceilings in others. At one point he staggered backwards a little, cursing and rubbing at his hand.

"What is it, baby?" Sherry asked, concerned.

"I don't know," he replied, shining his light on the spot his hand had just been. "You know how something can be so hot it's almost cold? That's what this wall felt like. I don't see nothing, though."

Sherry experimented and placed her own hand on the wall. The stones underneath it were jagged and cold and maybe just a little damp. But there was something else, too. A drumming sensation appeared under her palm, like she'd swallowed her heart and it had gone straight to her hand. She could almost see her hand moving up and down over the stones, a rhythmic tremor. Then she realized it wasn't coming from her hand at all, but from the wall.

Sherry quickly brought her hand back to her chest and folded it up. For a moment she'd been sure the wall had a heartbeat and was pulsating. But that was crazy, right?

"I can't find nothing," Brian finally sighed. "I'll take a walk around outside but if the sewer is leaking it's not down here. No dead animals, either."

Brian went up first and Sherry followed him. With her back to the room she felt vulnerable and exposed and was never so glad to emerge into the bright and sunny kitchen.

Day 3

Jenny woke up violently ill on the third day of Laura's absence.

She was projectile vomiting and running a fever so high that Mary wondered if they shouldn't take her the E.R.

"I'll be okay," Jenny said weakly. She was sitting on the bathroom floor, her back resting on the claw foot tub and her hand on the toilet bowl. She'd spent all morning in there, unable to leave thanks to the alternating between having diarrhea and vomiting.

"You sure you don't want me to run you a bath or something?" Mary asked. She wished Laura was there. Laura would've known what to do.

"No, I'm okay. I don't think I could sit up in one. But keep Candy away from me, will you? I don't want her getting sick too."

With two sick parents who couldn't do much Mary was now the adult of the household. She burnt the toast and bacon and made the eggs too runny for breakfast. She failed getting Candy dressed because she was unable to find the Alf shirt she wanted to wear. Unable to get the kids to make their own beds, she did it for them.

The rest of the kids did behave well, however, as though they needed to be extra cautious with the adults in the house being in bed. After Mary shooed them outside to play she straightened up the living room and kitchen, trying to remember how Laura polished the furniture and dusted them the right way. Jimmy hadn't even gotten up that morning and she took the opportunity to change the sheets on the couch where he'd been spending so much time. They were filthy and smelled like a combination of sweat and urine which made her feel even sorrier for her dad.

Once she got them in the washing machine Mary made some Jell-O from a packet and put it in the refrigerator to set. She took up glasses of orange juice and bottles of Ale-8s, but neither Jimmy nor Jenny were able to drink them.

Mary held Jenny's hair back while she vomited and then wet a washrag and wipe down her forehead. Jenny was pale and weak, her lips dry and cracked. She looked like she might have the flu or a very bad case of food poisoning. Mary was finally able to help her back to bed and, there, she tucked her in and smoothed back her hair as though Jenny were a child herself.

Content that she'd done everything she could possibly do, Mary went outside to play with the others.

Suppertime came and went. Mary was able to open two cans of tuna and make Tuna Helper, her favorite. They followed it with watermelon. Mary was getting nervous, however, because their food supply was low. They barely had any milk left and after tomorrow they'd be out of eggs. There were just a few potatoes in the bin and they'd all grown large eyes. Someone would have to go to the store soon but neither one of the adults could drive. She hoped her uncle would return the next day and take them all out. Jenn hadn't found a new job yet and Jimmy had called in sick five days in a row. If he didn't make it back to the car dealership where he worked as a mechanic soon they were going to fire him.

With all of these adult worries Mary was exhausted. When she took the Jell-O upstairs to her dad and Jenny, however, she felt ashamed. They were in much worse condition than she'd thought. Jenny wasn't even able to sit up in bed to eat, she was so weak and Jimmy had urinated in a cup next to the bed so that he didn't have to leave.

"I think you should try to go to the doctor tomorrow," Mary said as she spooned cherry Jell-O into Jenny's mouth. "You're likely to get dehydrated if you don't eat or drink nothing."

"I feel like my body's on fire," Jenny whispered. "Like I'm burning from the inside out. I keep dreaming that I'm being eaten alive by flames."

"It's the fever," Jimmy said, his voice tight with pain.

"I keep seeing things and hearing things," Jenny said again. "Things that aren't there."

Mary shivered and looked around. As it was dark out, she'd turned on a lamp in the corner but it did little to illuminate the room. The bedroom was still full of shadows and dark corners.

"What'd you see?" Mary asked, afraid of what the answer might be.

"There was a woman once," Jenny shuddered. "She walked to the window and just stood there. When she turned around she didn't have a face. I knew it was just a dream, probably 'cause of what Laura said, but it felt so real. And then these voices. Sometimes singing, sometimes...chanting," Jenny let her voice trail off and closed her eyes. "It reminded me of being in church."

Back in their bedroom Mary got the other girls tucked into bed and made a sleeping bag for Bobby on the floor. He didn't need to sleep with his parents that night. There was no use in him getting sick, too.

They'd all settled down and fallen asleep when a banging woke them up.

"Huh?" Brenda asked groggily, sitting up in the bed. Mary and Natalie awoke as well and Mary reached over to turn the light on. "What *is* that?"

"I think something fell," Natalie offered.

But then it came again, the thunderous knocking, loud enough to wake the dead. And it was at their bedroom door.

"That's not something falling," Mary cried, jumping to her feet. "That's our door."

Standing in the middle of the floor in her white flannel nightgown, her eyes wide with fear, Mary stared at their door, closed shut to keep the cool air in from the fan. Natalie climbed out of bed as well and stood next to her, slipping her small hand into her sister's. "Mary, who is it?" she whispered.

"I don't know," Mary whispered back.

It came again, then, the pounding rattling the pictures on the wall. Brenda shrieked and dove under the blanket, nothing but the top of her head peeking out.

"It might be Dad or Jenny needing something," Mary said uncertainly. "Maybe they're sicker now."

With cautious steps she walked to the door, dragging Natalie along with her. Her baseball bat was in the corner of the room and she went to it and picked it up, releasing Natalie and raising the bat in her hands. "You turn the knob and I'll be ready, okay?" she asked her. Natalie nodded.

On the soft count of "three" Natalie swung open the door and Mary jumped forward, ready to strike if necessary. The hall was lit up by a nightlight, but nobody was there.

Mary stepped out and looked in both directions. She didn't see a soul. The bathroom across from her was dark. She hadn't heard anyone running down the stairs or walking away at all, and the floorboards were creaky.

"I'm gonna go check on Dad," she said.

With speed she didn't know she possessed, Mary sprinted down the shadowy hallway and opened her dad's bedroom door.

Both adults were still in bed, light snoring telling her they were both asleep. The knocking had apparently not awoken them but it also meant that it wasn't them who did the knocking in the first place.

Next, Mary went back to her bedroom and grabbed the baseball bat again. "Stay up here," she hissed to the others. "I'm gonna check downstairs."

"I'm going with you," Brenda cried, jumping up from beneath the covers. "I'm not staying up here."

"Me too, me too," Natalie sang.

"No, one of you has to stay with Candy and Bobby," Mary said, casting a glance at her little brother who was curled up in a fetal position on the floor, staring wildly at the girls. Candy was still asleep.

Natalie opted to stay so Brenda and Mary took off downstairs, creeping silently down the staircase with their little girl feet barely making a sound.

Mary'd left a light on in the living room and for that she was thankful. Everything was in order. The front door was shut and when she tried the knob she found it locked. Nobody had made a mad dash out the door. When Mary opened the door she was met by the sounds of the cricket and tree frog orchestra, all singing loudly and off key. The night was somehow comforting, the big sky filled with stars and a bright shining moon. She so wanted to run out into the yard, sleep under the sky, and feel safe.

Going back into the house filled her with dread and she felt the fear wrap its arms around her and squeeze. She couldn't leave her sisters and brother.

Back upstairs she shut and locked the door. They kept the lamp on, but none of them were able to go back to sleep until daylight.

Day 4

The 4th day was blessedly quiet.

Jenny wasn't back to feeling 100% yet but she was able to get up and move around a little. Mary continued taking on the work Laura and Jenny would've done and let her rest as much as possible. She continued to worry about her father, however, because he didn't seem to be improving at all.

Jenny spent most of the day on the couch, watching soaps and talk shows. Mary scurried around, trying to throw food together for the younger ones and checking on her father throughout the day. She had little time to rest or play with so many people needing different things, but the work kept her mind busy.

She told Jenny about the banging on the door the night before but, as she suspected, Jenny hadn't heard it.

"You don't need to be up traipsing around investigating by yourself," Jenny admonished her. "You should've woke me up. What if it had been a crazy person?"

Mary shrugged. "I thought you needed the rest."

The fact was, a crazy person was somehow less frightening than what Mary knew it to truly be–a ghost or even a demon.

"We need to start praying more," Jenny declared. "That's the whole problem with this thing. We're just not praying enough. God might be punishing us by sending demons to us."

Mary didn't think God would do such a thing. Even though he was mighty and powerful she didn't think he could control the demons. Wasn't that supposed to be the devil's job? Still, it wouldn't hurt to pray more. She'd been praying in her head for the past few days. Tonight she'd make the little ones say bedtime prayers before going to sleep.

Mary's Uncle Brian and Aunt Sherry arrived around noon with their daughter June. June, affectionately known as "June Bug" was three years old. She was the life of the party whenever she was around and the girls always enjoyed having her over. When they'd arrived at the new house she'd immediately ran off to play with the others. Candy, in particular, was happy to have a playmate for the afternoon.

"So how's it going?" Brian asked. They were sitting on the front porch, as they usually did in the afternoon since it was so much cooler out there.

Jenny had shrugged, feeling more and more irritated by the minute. "I'm about ready to get out of here," she said. "Things are just getting to be too much for me."

"Can't though," Jimmy said weakly from the swing. He looked pale and bony. Brian later told him he looked like he'd aged fifteen years or more since the last time he'd seen him, just a couple of days before. "All our money's tied up in the move."

"If you need a place to stay, man, I'll find you one," Brian vowed.

"Naw, we'll be okay. Just some growing pains settling in here I guess," he scoffed.

Jenny did not look convinced. There was much she wanted to say but every time she'd brought it up it had started a fight. She knew they were broke, knew they'd spent all their money on the deposit and first month's rent (not to mention the gas moving their crap over there) and it would be months before they recouped any of that. Maybe longer if Jimmy didn't get back to work soon.

A few minutes later the kids came flying around the house, panting from exhaustion and excitement. "It's June Bug," Brenda gasped. She double over at the waist to catch her breath and pointed behind her.

Natalie, still running but a little slower, was pulling June Bug by the hand as she toddled behind. The adults were startled to see June Bug's face as white as a sheet, her eyes bulging, and her lips quivering like she had a chill.

"Baby! You okay?" Sherry jumped from her chair and was off the porch in seconds. Sprinting across the yard to her daughter she scooped her up and began whacking her on the back. "Is she choking? What'd she put in her mouth?" Sherry demanded, her own eyes wide with fright.

"Nothing," Natalie cried, tears running down her face in terror. "She just started making that noise."

"And her face turned all funny," Brenda added. She'd walked over to Natalie and grabbed her hand. Together, they watched in apprehension.

The gurgling sounds coming from June Bug's throat were unlike anything Mary had ever heard. As she gasped and wheezed and panted it *did* sound like she was choking.

Brian had joined his wife and daughter and was trying to open her mouth to look down her throat. He stuck his finger deep inside to dislodge whatever might be there and June Bug doubled over in pain, letting out a horrible scream that made them all jump a little. At last she stopped and fell limply against Sherry's side. Brian picked her up and carried her back to the porch swing where he sat down and began to rock her.

"What was wrong with her?" Sherry cried. Her fear and panic had given way to grief and the tears rolled down her cheeks in quick succession. "Is she gonna be okay?"

"It's probably this damn house," Jenny muttered, looking shaken herself. "I'd take her to your preacher and have him pray over her if I was you. We ought to do it to all of us. Especially Jimmy."

Jimmy looked on in grave concern, his eyes never leaving June Bug's tired little face. She looked like she'd been through a war. "It's not a bad idea," he agreed quietly. "Brian, you know we love you guys and I wouldn't say this if I didn't but..."

"What is it?" Brian asked, not looking up from his small daughter nestled in his arms.

"Don't come back here. We'll get out as soon as we can. I just don't want you coming back around. I'd probably kill myself if I thought something happened to you all."

Day 5

Jimmy was able to get out of bed again and walk around the house on the 5th day.

"These damn pills are making me sleep too much," he grumbled. "I gotta get back to work or they're gonna fire my ass."

"You need to go back to the doctor then and have 'em take a look at you," Jenny said. "Or at least go to the E.R. and see somebody else."

Jimmy's main bone of contention was that he didn't have any health insurance and couldn't pay for the E.R. "Oh, don't be dumb," Jenny chided him. "They got them programs at the hospital for us poor people. You wouldn't have to pay much, just fill out a bunch of papers."

So, everyone loaded up in the truck and Jenny took off down the road.

Jenny and Jimmy rode upfront, Jimmy's frail body wrapped in an afghan from the back of the couch. His head rested on the window, banging painfully on the glass whenever Jenny hit a pothole. She was still weak and sickly but could manage to drive alright.

The kids all rode in the truck bed, the girls' long hair flying out behind them as they sped down the road. Mary thought that being out in the truck, away from the house, was like a slice of heaven. As the wind whipped at her face and forced her eyes closed she opened her mouth to take in big gulps, feeling like she was feeding herself a fresh slice of sunshine. Surely nothing could hurt them now. The farther they got from the house, the better she felt.

Even Jimmy looked like he'd perked up a little when they arrived at the hospital. He was able to walk without any help and didn't grimace in pain as he slowly made his way through the E.R. doors and took a seat.

It took hours for the doctors to run their tests and check him out but nobody could find any answers. "You might just have some inflammation," the doctor said at last. All the kids were crowded into the exam room with Jimmy and Jenny. They were bored and tired but all were still in amazingly good spirits. Mary had cleaned out the truck and found a few dollars in change. They'd used it to buy all kinds of junk food from the vending machines and now, high on sugar, the kids were as content as they ever were.

"What can I do about inflammation doc?" Jimmy asked. Thanks to the morphine and Xanax he was feeling better than he had in more than a week.

"I can give you some stronger pain medication and that should help. Use it sparingly though," he cautioned. "Just take it when you feel the pain is coming on stronger. You should clear up in a few days."

Although they were down to their last little bit of money Jenny swung by the grocery store. By then she was too tired and weak to go in herself so she handed the wad of cash to Mary and told her to shop wisely. "You know what all we need. Don't buy a lot of junk," she said. As Mary started off with the others in tow she could still hear Jenny holler, "But don't forget the Ale-8s."

It turned out that twenty-five dollars didn't buy a whole lot of food for seven people. She managed to load up on spaghetti potatoes, milk, eggs, and bread though and that would last them for awhile. The kids were getting cranky, with Candy and Bobby crying for candy bars and colas by the time they left. Even though Mary had snapped at them more than once and was nervous about not having enough money on her she was still feeling better than she did inside their house. She hated to go home.

From the outside, their house looked the same. The only thing different was that Lulu was pacing slowly back and forth in front of the porch, growling lowly and shaking her head from side to side.

"You think she's hurt?" Bobby asked, afraid to get too close to her.

"I don't think so," Jenny replied weakly. "Probably after a rabbit or something trapped under the porch. Mary, can you bring the groceries in? I'm too tired."

Mary noticed the note sticking on their front door first. "Daddy, somebody left something here for us."

"What is it baby?" he asked. He'd slumped into the swing, too tired to make it on inside just yet.

Mary took the note from the door and opened it up. "It's from Uncle Brian," she said and began reading to herself.

A few lines into it she let out a horrible, strangled sound and let the note drop from her fingers. The others watched it as it floated to the ground like a feather. Mary stood still, her hands covering her mouth, her eyes wide.

"What is it?" Jenny asked, on the verge of exasperation.

"It's-it's-" Mary couldn't get the words out. Saying them would make it real.

Bending over with effort, Jenny picked the sheet of paper up and began reading it aloud.

"Stopped by but you were out. June Bug was hit by a car in the road today. Spent all day in the hospital but she didn't make it. Please call. Sherry needs you guys right now. Love, Brian."

Jimmy let out a noise that sounded like something between a sob and a scream. It got lost in his throat and when he swallowed it, it tore an awful hole in his stomach. Bending over from the pain he began to weep loudly, pulling at his hair and stomping his feet on the ground.

Mary and Brenda fell to the dirt and clung to each other, crying aloud. Tears were not enough. Natalie, stunned, quietly turned and walked to the big tree. Nobody said anything as she climbed to the top.

"That baby?" Bobby whispered. "That little baby's dead?"

"Who dead Mommy? Who dead?" Candy clambered onto the porch and pawed at Jenny's jean shorts.

"It's okay baby," Jenny cried as she reached down and scooped her little one up. She held her tightly, drawing in a whiff of her baby scent and burying her head in her hair. "It's okay."

Together they stayed outside, crying and whispering amongst themselves. June Bug was barely three years old. They lived on a road with hardly any traffic and had been there for years. Why now? None of them wanted to think about the awful noises she'd made the day before, or how Jimmy had pressed them to go to their preacher.

Still in shock, it was Mary who finally remembered the groceries. "I'd better get the milk and beef inside before it spoils," she whispered about an hour later.

Jenny nodded numbly. "Guess we'd better go back out in a little bit and head over to Sherry's," she said without any emotion.

Mary tried to imagine what she'd say to her aunt and uncle when she saw them, what she'd feel when she saw the little casket of her cousin. She'd never been to a kid's funeral before. She knew that kids died but they weren't supposed to. Jesus was supposed to protect the little kids.

Jenny and Jimmy headed on into the house, leaving Mary to organize the kids. She handed each one a bag and then hopped from the truck bed, trying to figure out what she could make for dinner. She knew they *had* to eat, even if they didn't feel like it now.

As the last one in the house, she was the last to see what had happened. She'd thought nothing else could possibly go wrong, not with the news of June Bug's death. She was wrong.

The others stood in stunned silence, staring at the middle of the floor. The kids had dropped their bags and now a can of corn was rolling towards the staircase. "Be careful," she snapped, reaching for the carton of eggs from Bobby and hoping none of them had broken.

But then she stopped when she saw what they were all looking at.

The gold and wooden crosses were no longer on their respective walls. Instead, they were lying in the middle of the floor, broken in half. In their place was a smear of red, thick and shiny.

Mary watched as it ran down the wall, leaving a line of scarlet behind, and pooled on the floor below.

The crosses weren't the only things to suffer, however. Last year a bunch of boys in Mary's class had gotten in trouble for making spit wads and throwing them on the ceilings. She remembered how those wadded up papers looked like rough snowballs. Now it looked like the living room floor was littered with them. The paper was everywhere-on top of the television, on the couch, on the bottom stairs, and all over the floor.

When she reached down and picked one up close to her shoe she carefully smoothed it out. She read aloud the first thing that caught her eye: "Put on the full armor of God, so that you will be able to stand firm against the schemes of the devil. Ephesians 6:11."

It was then that everyone realized that the shredded terrible mess they were standing in was the pages from their family Bible.

"Vandals," her father spat in disgust. "Some damn kids coming in and trying to make trouble."

Mary remembered his words much later that night as she lay there in the dark, trying hard to fall asleep. They'd spent the evening at her aunt and uncle's house, doing their best to console them. She'd helped clean their bathroom while Natalie and Brenda had picked up the living room and vacuumed, getting ready for the guests they were sure to have. Everyone had moved like a robot, nobody saying much of anything. The grown-ups' eyes were all dull and almost scary looking. She didn't like looking at them. Sherry had sat in the corner of the living room, holding June Bug's teddy bear to her chest. She still had some faint streaks of blood across her arm but she wouldn't let anyone wash it off of her.

And now, at night, she thought about their living room. Her father firmly believed that some kids had broken in, slapped some paint on the floor and torn things up. She wanted to think he was right, wanted to believe that it was some*one* who had done those things and not some*thing*.

But she didn't know. The stuff on the wall hadn't looked like any kind of paint she'd ever seen before. She'd never seen those kinds of symbols or words either. They looked like something she'd seen in her history book from Egypt or something. As she'd scrubbed at it with a sponge it had sprang a sickly tart smell, something she recognized but couldn't put her finger on. Her tummy had gone a little funny then and she'd almost thrown up. Brenda wouldn't get anywhere near it, although Candy was mighty interested and kept toddling over and trying to touch it with her chubby fingers. Mary had shooed her away more than once, horrified at what might happen if it got on her baby sister.

Natalie's warm body beside her was comforting. Her breath was soft and the rise and fall of her body made Mary feel less alone. She hated being the only one awake but she didn't want to waken the others. She could tell that she was the only one in the house awake. Sometimes at night she could hear her parents whispering down the hall. They used soft voices to keep the others from hearing but their voices still carried through the old walls. And sometimes she could hear the squeaks of their bedsprings. It embarrassed Laura to hear it but Mary didn't mind. To her it meant they loved each other and were happy and that's what mattered most. (Not that she ever wanted to walk in on it and see it, like Natalie had done once.)

Tonight the whole house was quiet and there wasn't a single sound other than their fan, not even the chirping of a cricket or the flutter of bat wings against the windows. They'd put up some wax paper where the glass was broken and the bats seemed to like that. They were always flying up against it and trying to poke their way through it.

Mary was just about asleep, somewhere in that twilight period, when a sound in the darkness wakened her. The room was pitch black, the moon hidden by the clouds and blocking out any light. The fan whirled at the foot of their bed, a rhythmic sound that Mary kind of liked. That wasn't what woke her up, though.

Somewhere over by the other bed currently occupied by Brenda and Candy was a humming noise, like the VCR was overheating and needed to be turned off. Mary propped herself up on her elbows and looked around, her eyes straining in the dark. She couldn't see a darn thing, not even the outlines of Candy and Brenda.

"Brenda," she whispered loudly. "*Brenda*, do you hear that?"

Brenda stirred in her sleep and groaned. Mary's stuffed teddy bear was still in bed with her. She could hardly sleep without it, even though she knew it was kind of babyish. Picking him up now she tossed him hard in Brenda's direction.

"Hey," Brenda yelped. Mary could hear the covers rustling and knew Brenda was awake now. "What did you do *that* for?"

"Just listen," Mary hissed. "Do you hear that?"

Both girls were quiet, tuning their ears to the sound. The hum rose louder now, whirring and droning forcefully. "What *is* that?" Brenda asked, her voice shaking. Mary could hear the fear rising in her voice and felt a little guilty for waking her up.

"Did you leave something plugged in?" Mary asked.

"No!"

Suddenly, the humming stopped and they were left with nothing but the sound of the fan. Mary was able to fall back to her pillow when Brenda gasped and then moaned a little.

Although the room was still as dark as it could be, two red lights materialized by the chest of drawers by Brenda and Candy. They were faint at first, two pinpricks that were barely distinguishable. Mary thought her eyes might be playing tricks on her so she closed them and scrubbed her hands over them. When she opened them, however, the lights were still there and they seemed to be directed at the girls' beds. As the girls watched in dismay the tiny lights grew brighter and more intense, seemingly hovering in midair. The scarlet lights bore into them, slicing through Mary and making her tingle deep inside. She could feel her heartbeat quicken, her skin grow hot, and a sharp pain digging into her stomach. The hairs on her head were moving, like something was crawling through it and she frantically raked her hands through her curls in an attempt to get it out.

"Eyes, it's eyes," Brenda shrieked. Panicked, Brenda jumped from her bed and ran, stumbling in the darkness and landing on Bobby, waking him.

"Hey," he cried. "Get off me."

Brenda sniveled and cried but Mary couldn't take her eyes from the lights. They *did* look like eyes and they were looking right back at her. Nearly frozen in fear now she tried to get up but couldn't. She was rooted to her mattress, bound to Natalie's sleeping figure. Feeling as though she had no other options left, she silently began praying to herself. "Our father, who art in Heaven, hallowed be thy name..."

Across from her, Candy began making the horrible gurgling sound that June Bug had made just the day before.

Brenda cried out again, this time a muffled sound as though her head was buried in a blanket.

With new strength, Mary spoke her words aloud now. On and on she repeated the prayer as quickly as she could, saying the words over and over again by instinct. Her heart pounding, sweat rolling down her face, she forced herself to continue, to pray away whatever was there in the room with them. Something was squeezing her chest in a vise but she ignored it and focused on breathing in and out. She could feel the air around her change, grow thicker and darker. Candy continued to choke and gurgle, fighting against whatever was hovering over her. Something continued to probe at Mary, prickling at her mind as though trying to get inside. Her scalp still tingling like there were a million little bugs crawling around through her hair but she refused to touch it, instead keeping her hands clasped tightly in front of her.

Brenda and Bobby began praying along with her now, their voices blending together and touching one another in the darkness. They were linked even though they couldn't see one another. Hearing her brother and sister gave Mary extra strength and so she prayed louder, staring at the two lights as she did so. Their voices swelled and filled the room, waking Natalie who sat up in bed in confusion and then gasped when she saw the crimson glows. She buried her head under the covers and wrapped her skinny arms around Mary's waist, burrowing as deeply into the bed as she could. Their voices carried down the hallway where they woke Jimmy and Jenny. Mary could hear them rushing towards their bedroom door but she forced the sounds out, intent on her prayers.

It couldn't have been more than a minute or two that passed but they would all later say it felt like an eternity. When she thought she couldn't stand another moment without screaming, the bedroom door flew open, the air around her cleared and the bloodshot beams disappeared, fading into the night.

Day 6

Mary was the first one up.

She slid out of bed, got dressed, and made her way downstairs. It was earlier than she usually woke up and the dew was still on the grass when she went out to feed Lulu. For a moment she stood on the porch and let the cool air wrap itself around her. Gentle fog was rolling off the fields as the sun burnt it away. Off in the distance she could see cows grazing and a farmer pulling his tractor across a field. It really was pretty out there where they lived and the house was just the right size. If only it weren't so dang scary.

Jenny got up next, but Mary had already started breakfast. Letting her do the work, Jenny sat down at the table, her hands wrapped around a hot cup of coffee. She looked tired and fifteen years older but at least she could keep food down now.

"I'm worried about your daddy," she said at last. "He just ain't doing so good."

"What do you think it is?" Mary asked, popping bread in the toaster.

"I think it's this house is what I think. It got his back and it made me sick. I don't want it getting to you kids next."

Mary shuddered. She thought about telling Jenny what happened the night before but she didn't even want to think about that. She was trying to forget it ever happened. Natalie, Brenda, and Bobby came down later, just a few minutes apart. The kids all sat down around the table, waiting patiently for their food. Nobody spoke.

Finally, Jenny looked at them and asked, "Where's Candy?"

"She's still in bed asleep," Brenda answered. "I tried to wake her up but she wouldn't."

A flash of fear shot through Jenny's eyes. In what looked like one fluid movement she was up on her feet and flying through the rooms. Mary could hear her taking the stairs two at a time. Beating herself up for not checking on Candy before she came downstairs, Mary slumped against the refrigerator door. What if Candy was hurt or sick? What if she was…dead? Little kids like that couldn't just die in their sleep could they?

Fear grew sickeningly in her belly and acrid bile rose up her throat. She gagged on it a little and then spat it out in the sink. Visions of Candy, blue and cold, danced in her head. Her little sister could be a pain, but she loved her.

When Jenny appeared what felt like hours later, Mary was relieved to see Candy in her arms. Her eyes were open and she was alert, scanning the room and letting her gaze land on each of her siblings.

Jenny, however, was pale. Her eyes were bright and shiny and her lips trembled as she sat Candy down at the table. Mary noticed a long, thin scratch on Jenny's cheek then. It was oozing blood in little droplets and running down to her jawline.

"What happened? Are you okay?" Mary asked, reaching for a piece of paper towel.

"Candy did it," Jenny replied. She took the offered paper and dabbed at her cheek, leaving a smear of blood behind. "Just reached out her hand and scratched me. I gave her a spanking but she never even cried."

"What did you do that for?" Mary asked Candy. The toddler gazed at her quizzically but did not answer. There was something different about her, something Mary couldn't put her finger on. Candy was usually bubbly, laughing and talking at the table and sometimes singing the Smurf song. Today she was quiet and reserved. Mary knew it was crazy but she thought Candy somehow looked older. But that didn't make any sense at all.

Candy remained silent while Mary ladled gravy over biscuits and slid scrambled eggs onto everyone's plates. She did not make a move to eat, however, and continued to stare at her siblings and mother, taking them all in one at a time. It was unnerving to Mary and even the younger ones were rattled by her intensity. "Stop it Candy," Bobby snapped. When he threw his napkin at her she let out a hissing sound and pretended to scratch at him with make-believe claws.

The others sat back in their chairs, forks held up in the air on the way to their mouths. Candy could be a pain but she wasn't a mean child. In fact, she was usually loving and gentle, always ready for a hug or kiss from anyone who would indulge her.

"Just leave her alone," Jenny said wearily. "We got enough trouble. I'll deal with her later."

When Jimmy staggered down, his eyes bloodshot and hair disheveled, he took nothing but plain toast. "Not feeling good again," he mumbled. "Might a gotten what you got, Jenny."

Candy turned her gaze on him and stared without blinking, causing him obvious discomfort. "Shit, Candy, what's the matter with you?"

She laughed then, a full-bodied laugh that was rich and deeper than her high-pitched toddler voice. The laugh rang out through the small kitchen, seemingly amplified. Mary gawked at her, her mouth slackened. "Candy?" she whispered but Candy just sneered.

With everyone watching she reached forward and grabbed the jar of grape jelly. Using her finger, she scooped up a clump of it and let it slide down her hand, staining her arm with purple. With a little "glop" it landed on the table.

"I drank their blood," she whispered in a voice that sounded neither her's nor human. "I drank *all* their blood."

"What?" Jenny asked. She tried to giggle but it sounded forced. "Are you teasing us?"

"No!" Candy snapped, leaning forward for more jelly. This time she stuck her entire hand in the jar and grabbed as much as she could. As she smacked her hands together the jelly squirted out everywhere, landing on the table, the floor, and in Natalie's hair.

"Hey!" Natalie yelped, jumping up from the table.

"I drank their blood," she said again, "and listened to them scream."

"Honey," Jimmy tried. "Did you get that from a movie?"

Candy turned her head swiftly to face him. "Noooo," she all but purred and then licked the jelly from her hands. "Robert Meadows died. I cut his throat with my knife and watched him bleed."

Candy giggled then, a sickening sound that bore into Mary's stomach. She thought she might vomit.

"I cut his throat and he bled for so long...And Pearl Ann Miller. I stabbed her chest and cut her hair. She screamed and died and I drank her blood, too."

White with horror, Jenny reached her arm out to touch Candy. "Candy," her voice trembled. "Where did you get that?"

Grabbing her fork Candy turned and dug it into her mother's hand as hard as she could. As Jenny cried out in pain,

Candy jumped up from the table and stood in her chair. On and on she laughed, even when Jimmy stepped forward and swatted her on the bottom. "That's enough of that," he yelled. "You stop that right now."

Candy moaned and shook her head as though to drown out his voice. "I killed Raymond Martin. I killed Randall Newman. I killed Polly Patrick. I killed them all and their blood was sweet!"

Brenda ran from the room then, muttering under her breath. Bobby was right behind her, mumbling "freak" as he passed by. Candy clapped her hands in delight. "You're all going to rot in hell, you're all going to suffer! The bastards tried to stop me but I didn't take their shit. They fucked with me and I fucked right back. Do you want me to fuck with you?" She stared into her father's eyes and held onto his gaze. He didn't waver but calmly held out his hand to Natalie who was standing closest to him.

"Get your clothes on and make sure the others are dressed. We're going out," he said softly, straightening his back as much as he could. "Jenny, go put your shoes on."

"Fucking whore!" Candy screeched, her voice shrill and crazed. "Fucking whore with the serpent between her legs!"

Jenny covered her mouth and choked back a muffled scream. With tears gathering in her eyes she ran from the room, Natalie with her.

"It's okay Jenny," Mary could hear Natalie soothing her in the other room. "She's just a little sick."

"'Sick'? You're all sick!" Candy purred. "Sick with the plague that runs through your souls!"

Mary closed her eyes and began praying, every prayer she'd ever known falling from her tongue. "Our father who art in Heaven, now I lay me down to sleep, Yea though I walk through the valley of the shadow of death," she couldn't remember her prayers but strung them together in a frantic hope that it would help.

"I laugh at prayers you whore!" Candy said. She picked up her plate and threw it violently to the floor, making it crash into dozens of pieces. The sound made Jimmy jump but he didn't move back.

"Go on and get your shoes on, baby," he said to Mary. "Wait with the others."

With her shoes on and the others dressed, Mary had all her siblings piled into the truck, waiting, when Jenny and Jimmy ran from the house. He'd wrapped a blanket around Candy, enclosing her small body as tightly as a burrito. Her arms and legs were trapped inside, unable to move, and she thrashed violently in Jimmy's arms, trying to escape. Despite his back he held onto her, keeping his face turned away so that it wouldn't be struck by her spitting.

Jenny drove while Jimmy sat in the passenger seat, doing his best to hold her powerful movements down. Even through the wind and the glass Mary could still hear her little sister screaming, sometimes talking gibberish and sometimes using curse words Mary herself didn't know.

She wasn't surprised when Jenny pulled up in front of their small Baptist church. Since it was Tuesday nobody was inside but the preacher lived next door in a little Bedford stone house. The kids waited while Jenny sprinted to the door and knocked. When there was no answer right away Jenny knocked again, this time with more force. She hopped from one foot to another, jittery with anticipation. When the slender elderly man opened his door, Mary could see that he was wearing a bathrobe. Although Mary couldn't hear them, she could see from the way Jenny waved her arms around and pointed to the truck that she was trying to make him understand the brevity of the situation. When he closed the door some minutes later and Jenny headed back to the truck Mary was sorely disappointed. She felt despair washing through her and wanted to fall over in tears. Surely if anyone could help them it would be her preacher. But he had left them alone, too. They would handle it all on their own and Mary didn't think she could bear that.

When Jenny opened the door, though, she said, "Bring her to the sanctuary. He'll meet us there."

Candy's screeching and hissing intensified when they stepped up on the porch of the tiny little white church. Jimmy looked pained and weary, as though his body would give out at any moment. Mary wanted to offer to help but knew she couldn't hold Candy on her own.

When the preacher unlocked the door and let them in Candy let out a wail that sliced through the air. The church bell above them began to move then, its steady tone drowning her out. Mary took a moment to savor that sweet reprieve and then followed her family into the sanctuary.

Reverend Loyal House was a no nonsense kind of man. He believed in the Old Testament and was as fire and brimstone as anyone could be. He didn't understand this new phase going on, where churches focused more on making people happy than putting the fear of God into them like they should be doing. He'd seen a lot in his fifty two years as a preacher. He seen his share of murders, suicides, divorces, addiction, and illness. He had never, however, seen anything like the sight in front of him.

He liked the little family, the kids with their beautiful blond hair, the parents hardworking and spirited. He knew people talked when Jimmy divorced his first wife and married Jenny, who already had a son of her own and still a teenager. A lot of folks didn't like Jenny. He, however, had respect for her. It couldn't be easy to marry a man who came with four kids of his own, much less take them on as hers and mother them. And he knew she did her best.

The children were always well-behaved at church. They dressed as well as they could in their hand-me-down clothes, scuffed secondhand shoes, and little dollar store purses. The girls had voices like angels and he could always pick them out when everyone was singing. They said "yes sir" and "no ma'am" and were always the first to volunteer if anyone needed anything.

Candy, being the youngest member of the congregation (at least until Suzy Mays had her baby in the fall) was babied and petted on by half the members of the church. She was always ready with a big grin and hug for anyone who approached her.

The family who stood before him, however, was something else. Candy's sweet face had been replaced by a distorted one, a face raging with anger and madness. Her lips sneered, she panted and hissed as her eyes darted around the room, taking in the crosses and stained glass windows depicting the apostles. Jimmy was almost unrecognizable with the dark circles under his eyes, the sunken cheeks, and weight loss. His clothes hung on him like a scarecrow. Even the children were pale, their beautiful hair brittle and lank. They looked like a band of orphans, all hope and faith gone.

"Can you help us?" Brenda asked pitifully. "Please?"

The others nodded their heads.

"Sit down please," he gestured to the pews. They all obeyed promptly, turning their eyes on him in expectation. The pleading looks on their faces shook him to the core. He squeezed the Bible in his right hand a little harder. "Now, tell me what's been going on."

For the next fifteen minutes Jimmy and Jenny told Reverend House about their new home and the strange occurrences that had been happening since they moved in. They talked about the woman Laura had seen, the scent coming from the cellar, the red stain in the floor, the Bible being destroyed, the broken crosses, and Lulu getting trapped downstairs. However, they also spoke of things that the children didn't know anything about.

"A few days ago, Reverend, I was laying there on the couch trying to get some rest. The kids were all outside playing. I was kind of dozing off and on and then I heard something, something in the kitchen," Jimmy said. "It sounded like scratching, like maybe a dog or cat trying to dig something up. But then, well, then I knew it wasn't."

"What happened?" the Reverend prodded gently.

"I could hear the table moving. I knew that's what it was. I raised up and looked in the kitchen and there was the table, rocking back and forth. The linoleum was moving, too, like someone was under the trapdoor and trying to push their way out. It lasted for a minute or two and then stopped. And then I heard…" Jimmy stopped and took a breath before continuing. "I heard crying. Loud crying, like someone's heart was broken. I couldn't stand it. I ended up going outside with everyone else."

"I've been hearing and seeing stuff too," Jenny explained. "Sometimes just out of the corner of my eye, you know? It will fly by fast as lightning. Sometimes it's a woman, sometimes a man. Once it was even a kid. And the chanting, oh God the chanting. It keeps me up at night."

Mary sat back in bewilderment. Chanting? She'd never heard that. She was suddenly glad for the white noise her fan made.

"And now your little one," Reverend House added.

They all nodded.

"I have to tell you folks, this is unorthodox for me. I am not an exorcist, I can't perform miracles. For that we have to turn to the good Lord. However, I believe you when you say there's something wrong in your home. I can smell it even now. It's clinging to you and your clothing. I can offer a prayer for you, and lead you in prayer right now."

Mary nodded her head emphatically. Surely, with a preacher praying, everything would change for the better.

Reverend House had them all get in a circle around Jimmy and Candy. They held hands and bowed their heads as he began to lead them in prayer. His voice was low at first, barely more than a whisper. Candy was still for the first time since Jimmy picked her up, interested in what was going on.

As his voice rose, however, and echoed through the small church she began to thrash again, crying, "No! I'm burning," and banging her head against her father's chest. Mary felt tears rolling down her cheeks, the thought of her baby sister hurting, but she continued to pray, to hold tightly to the hands of Natalie and Brenda, as the Reverend droned on.

On and on he prayed, his voice ringing in a sing song pattern, a song or chant of redemption. He prayed for grace, for peace, for the deliverance of evil. He prayed for safety and hope. Jenny and Jimmy followed him with his "amens" and Jenny cried out at one point, moved to tears by the way peace began to fill her heart. Candy thrashed again, moaning and crying and begging everyone to stop, sometimes calling for her mommy and other times her daddy. Jimmy kept a firm grip on her, however, and rocked her back and forth, cooing to her softly.

And then, just as Mary thought Candy's cries couldn't get any louder, they did. With one final shout she screamed into the sanctuary, causing the silver collection plate to rattle and fall from its shelf. Mary shook and tried to cover her ears but Brenda and Natalie held onto her tightly.

The scream carried on and on, as though Candy might never run out of air. Mary imagined it could be heard everywhere, ringing out through the countryside like a warning bell. She sobbed aloud then, feeling ashamed and scared. The sound of Candy's cry was a primeval one, barely human.

And then, it stopped.

Candy fell limply against her father, her small mouth open in an "o." Mary dared a peek at her. She'd changed drastically, the soft light coming back into her eyes. Her lips were pink again instead of white, and there was a small smile playing upon them. The rush of relief Mary felt was overwhelming. She knew, then, that Candy would be okay.

"Let us sing," Reverend House commanded and they all joined into three versus of "Old Rugged Cross."

Day 7

"*We have to know what's going on here*," Jimmy said as he paced back and forth in front of the couch.

Jenny nodded and stroked Candy's hair. Candy hadn't gotten far from her mother in the past day and a half. She was always a little clingy to start with but since her ordeal she'd become even more so.

"I'm gonna go talk to some neighbors, see what I can find out," Jimmy declared. "If we knew what we were dealing with here we might be able to fix it."

Mary wasn't so sure about that. She just wanted out, forget "fixing" the house. "Can I go with you Daddy?"

"Yes, pumpkin, you can ride with me."

With more vigor in his step than she'd seen in a week, Jimmy hopped up into the cab of the truck. She slid in beside him and they started off down the road. The first house they stopped at was a little brick ranch, about a quarter of a mile from their house.

The woman who opened the door was middle aged and had two toddlers clinging to her skirt. Her hair was long, down to her waist, and her denim skirt made Mary think she was one of those Pentecostals or "Holy Rollers" as her daddy called them.

"Hi, ma'am, my name is Jimmy and I live down the road from you in that white farmhouse. This here's my daughter Mary," he began.

The woman looked at them with interest but didn't budge from the door.

"I was wondering if you knew anything about that house," he said. "Any history of it? We're having some, er, problems."

"No, sorry," she shook her head. "I just moved in here myself about a year ago."

The next two houses they tried didn't have anyone home.

Mary could tell that Jimmy was tired and growing frustrated. When they pulled up in front of another big white farmhouse, however, she could see an elderly couple on the porch. Oh please let them know something, she prayed.

Jimmy introduced himself again and went into his spiel. When he was finished the old man in overalls glanced over at his wife and then back up at Jimmy. "You mean Turner's?"

"Turner's what?" Jimmy asked in confusion. "The landlord's name is Estes I believe."

"Yeah, that's it," the old man agreed. "But back when it was a home it was Turner's."

"A home for what?" Mary ventured.

The old woman was stringing beans, her hands moving in a steady rhythm as she slid the strings down, snapped them in half, and threw them in a Tupperware bowl.

"Funeral home," the man replied. "Turner's Funeral Home."

"No, that must be something else," Jimmy said. "This is a house we live in. It's just a regular house."

"Big staircase inside? Barn out back? Big tree in the front yard?" the man asked.

Jimmy nodded. "Well, yeah."

"Yep. That was the funeral home."

"Are you sure about that?" Mary whispered, feeling the blood rush from her face.

"Been to many a funeral there," the woman said. It was the first time she'd spoken. "Place shut down, oh, I'd say about ten years ago. For a long time that house was empty."

"All kinds of things going on in that old house," the man agreed. "Kids used to sneak in there, have their satanic rituals, talk to the devil. Trying to conjure up their demons. Police run lots of 'em out, carrying their candles and Wee-jee boards with 'em."

Stunned, Jimmy and Mary looked at one another. "Well, that ain't the only thing about that old place," Mary said after a moment. "It's pretty close to the mound."

"What mound?" Jimmy asked.

"This whole area," the man gestured with his hands, "was a big Indian village. One of the only ones in the state. There's some spiritual rings and Indian mounds, gravesites, all over the place. Biggest one is just behind that house. Lots of fighting between the white man and Indians here, uh huh," the man nodded. "No telling what all you see and hear."

After thanking them for their time, Jimmy led Mary back to the truck. "Indian burial mounds and funeral homes? You've gotta be shittin' me."

Mary shivered, unable to believe it herself.

Her daddy went on a tear when he got back to the house. "Start packin', Jenny," he bellowed before he was even all the way inside. "Go get them boxes we were gonna burn from the barn. We're leaving."

"Why?" Jenny jumped up from the couch where she'd been taking a nap. "Where we going?"

"I don't know yet," Jimmy admitted, "but I'll figure it out. Don't worry. Just get the kids started."

Once they'd all hauled the boxes in from the barn and had sorted through them Jimmy left again. He was gone for awhile but when he got back his face was grim.

"Well, the good news is that Brian has a place for us, that trailer in town he rents out. People just moved yesterday and he hadn't even put it in the paper yet. Bad news is that the landlord's pretty pissed and won't give us back our deposit."

Jenny's face fell at the thought of going back to another trailer but anywhere had to be better than where they were. "How we gonna move without the deposit?"

"When I told him what was going on he said to just move on in, that we'd worry about paying him next month," Jimmy said. "To be honest, he wasn't shocked. Said he and Sherry had gotten a bad feel from the place themselves and almost said something to us. Wish they had now."

Mary and her sisters were upstairs throwing their clothes and toys into boxes from Kroger and Walmart when they heard the car pull up out front. A skinny man in a baseball hat and dirty jeans got out and marched up to the porch. Within minutes they could hear their father's voice ringing through the walls.

"What's he saying?" Brenda asked, walking to the bedroom door and straining her ears.

"I don't know," Mary answered back.

With Mary leading the way, the kids tiptoed down the stairs and stopped at the bottom. Their father was standing in the middle of the living room floor, gesturing wildly to the man in front of him. The man's face was red, like it might explode, but he wasn't saying anything.

Mary slid down and sat on the bottom stair, pressing her face through the spindles in the bannister. The others did the same. Nobody seemed to notice they were there.

"A funeral home!" Jimmy was shouting. "You put a bunch of little kids in a goddamned *funeral* home?"

"It was a house before it was a funeral parlor," the man said weakly, unable to match Jimmy's temper. "It's a good house, big enough for you and all your babies."

"Yeah, and whatever the hell else lives here. Big enough for the kids, big enough for the haints, big enough for the damned demons. Hell, it's big enough for all of us. One big happy family!"

Mary bit her lip to suppress a giggle.

"Look, nobody's ever complained before," the man argued. "Others have lived here."

"Yeah, for how long?" Jimmy demanded.

When the man didn't answer right away Jimmy laughed, a dry brittle sound. "Ha! That's what I thought. And you never stopped to think there might be something wrong with it?"

"Look, I ain't giving you your deposit back. You signed a lease for six months. You ought to be glad I'm not gonna charge you for the next five months, as is my legal right. We have a contract," he said prissily.

"Well I'll tell you what you can do with your goddamned contract," Jimmy sputtered. "You can shove it up your–"

Brenda coughed then and both men looked over at the staircase. The sight of the five young children with their hollow eyes and pale skin sitting bunched together on the stairs must have done something to the man because the red drained from his face and he managed to look ashamed.

"Well, it don't matter," he said at last. "I'll find somebody to rent it. It's a good house."

And with that, he sailed out the door.

"Keep packing kids," Jimmy said. "Keep packing."

They didn't stop.

Back with Laura

"And then we left," Natalie said. "We got up real early that next morning. Uncle Brian and Aunt Sherry brought a U-Haul and their pickup and we left. We didn't even go to bed that night."

"Fastest move I ever done," Jenny muttered. "Didn't even get a chance to clean it."

"We needed out of there," Jimmy explained. "Just as fast as we could do it."

My mother and I, who had sat there in silence while they took turns telling their tale, didn't know how to reply. We were speechless.

Laura left to get something from the kitchen and when she came back Jimmy pulled her down to his lap and gave her a squeeze. "So you can see why we wanted you to keep this one. No need for her to suffer along with the rest of us."

Laura snuggled into her father's shoulder and sighed.

"Daddy, we don't never have to go back there do we?" Brenda asked. Bobby's little face filled with horror at the thought and he shook his head vehemently and covered his eyes.

"I can promise you we will *never* ever go back. Or live in anything like that again," Jimmy swore. "I will *always* protect my babies."

The kids all gazed adoringly at him, trust in their eyes. The gold cross above the couch glittered in the sunlight.

Now

Fifteen years passed from the moment they moved out of the house to the next chapter of the story.

Although the children never returned to the house, not even for the few things they accidentally left behind in the rush, we continued to talk about it. As the years went by Natalie and Brenda forgot many of the things that happened. Candy, of course, was thankfully too little to remember *her* ordeal and can recall nothing of ever having lived there.

I didn't forget.

When I thought of being scared, I would always think of Laura's house and what went on there. It seemed to affect me as much, or even more than it did Laura who tried to move past it all and consider it nothing more than a bad dream.

For Laura, the majority of those two weeks were spent with me. That time for her was trying on bathing suits, walking to the mall to get banana splits, sneaking into "Far and Away" and giggling at the bowl over Tom Cruise's private parts. She didn't live the horror the rest of her siblings saw, but I believe a part of her always felt guilty that she wasn't there to protect them. Laura was, and still is, a mothering type.

Why didn't the others come home with me? I don't know. Perhaps at that point it was because Laura had seen the most.

She'd felt the push from behind while carrying the mattress. She'd seen the woman in the bathroom, had been locked in her own bedroom...The younger ones might not have had a good grasp of what was going on until much later.

At the age of twenty-six I lived two counties over from the farm house in the country and was working as a family therapist. On one particularly slow afternoon a group of my co-workers and I were sitting in my office, swapping stories about our childhoods.

Dena, a woman my age and not someone I knew well, caught everyone's attention when she spoke up and said, "Well, when *I* was a kid we lived in a haunted house. Anyone want to hear about that?"

Of course everyone wanted to know the details so we sat in rapturous attention while she told us of the disembodied voices at night, the plodding of men's work boots up and down the stairs, their Bibles and crucifixes destroyed or covered with pieces of paper...

A small bell began ringing in the back of my head but I ignored it. Laura's house was more than two hours away, in a tiny town that nobody had ever heard of. Dena wasn't even from that county. Surely most haunted houses had the same stories anyway. It *had* to be a coincidence.

"And then there was the embalming table in the basement," she shuddered. "I mean, how were *we* to know we'd rented a funeral parlor?"

There was no denying it then.

"Dena," I began with excitement, nearly falling out of my chair. "Can you tell me anything about the kitchen?"

"Sure," she shrugged, looking at me a little oddly. "It had a trapdoor going down to the cellar and this big red stain that we couldn't get clean. My mom always thought it was blood. Probably was."

In stunned silence I let the memories of Laura's house wash over me. Somehow the house had come back around to me, more than fifteen years later and through someone I barely knew in a county that didn't even contain the house.

I then proceeded to describe the rest of the floorplan to her, the best climbing tree in the front yard, the barn in the back...

As Dena listened her mouth dropped open slightly. "So you lived there too?" she asked in bewilderment.

"Not me, but my friend. They only stayed two weeks, though. The ghosts were too much for them."

"Well thank God," she swore. "You know, part of us always wondered if we were overacting and just hearing things. Finally, after all these years, I can go back to my mom and tell her that we weren't crazy after all."

Several years later I posted bits of both of their experiences online. Although I didn't offer the address, I *did* give the name of the small town it was in and described the house. As luck would have it, someone who lived in a farm nearby saw my posting. Excited, he traveled over to his neighbor's house and knocked on the door, ready to tell the owner stories about their home.

They were not amused.

There was something else about his visit that perplexed him and he felt he had to share it with me.

"What year and month did your friend live there?" he asked me in an email.

When I told him the dates of Laura's residency, he wrote me back. "It can't be that house, then. The person who lives there has been there twenty years. She's never rented it out."

Figuring he must have gone to a different house, I had him take a picture of the one he visited. He did so and sent it to me. There was no doubt about it, it was the same house. We continued to write back and forth, trying to solve this frustrating mystery.

"Maybe it was the one next door," he finally offered. He took a picture of it and sent it to me as well. Although there were some similarities, the house next door had certain architectural elements that I didn't remember Laura's house possessing. In addition, it lacked a front porch and there was no barn in the back.

Still, it *had* been a long time ago and my memory wasn't what it had once been. I sent both images to Dena and asked her to pick out the one she'd lived in.

"It's definitely the first one," she said in her reply, picking out the one I believed it to be as well. "The other one looks like a barn and I would definitely remember having lived in a barn."

I showed both images to Laura as well and she also picked out the same house.

I didn't press the issue with the gentleman any further but the exchange continues to bother me. Was the woman lying, forgetting when she moved in, or was something else going on? If she had indeed lived there for twenty years then neither Laura nor Dena could have rented it. Yet they both had. I knew Laura had lived there at least; we'd been to the house several times and watched them move in.

A few weeks later my husband and I went for a drive to see if I could find it again. As we neared the main road I had him slow down. "What's that sign marker say?" I asked, rolling down my window and straining my eyes to get a better look.

"There was an Indian village here," he summarized. "One of the only ones in the state. This whole area was a Native American town, more or less."

"I didn't think Indians really *lived* in Kentucky," I mused. "I thought they just came here to hunt and stuff."

"More and more evidence supports the fact that there were at least two main settlements here," my Anthropologist husband confirmed. "This was apparently one of them."

I thought about that as we continued down the long stretch of country road. A settlement meant Indian burial grounds, maybe even a skirmish. Who knew what all had gone on in the area.

Soon, we passed the house the man had thought it could be, the one with the barn-like roof. "That's not it," I said as we slowed down in front of it. "Laura's house had a big yard. This one is almost touching the road."

On down the road I had him slow down again. "There," I pointed, "*that's* it!"

The house had changed very little. It still had the barn in the back, the long gravel driveway, the big front porch, and the big yard. The climbing tree, however, was gone.

As I whipped out my camera to take a quick shot before we sped away I could see a large black Labrador. He was digging frantically by the small window at the side of the house, clawing at the dirt as though his life depended upon it.

Why?

Everyone wants "answers," including me. *Why* was the house haunted? *What* was haunting it? Was it a disgruntled ghost? A demon? Leftover energy from another time? How have other people been able to live in it with presumably little spiritual activity? Why was Dena's family able to live in it *longer* (a year) than Laura's?

I have several theories about the conditions surrounding the house that led to spiritual activity. Some of them are well documented.

Both families were informed that the house had once been a funeral home. I haven't been able to find any information to verify this, including through property records. The house as an alleged former funeral home probably had something to do with the negative energy that surrounded it, however, if that is indeed true. If it wasn't a funeral home then the table in the cellar remains unexplainable. I ventured to the cellar myself and saw the table and up close it definitely didn't look like a regular work table up close. It had a hole at either end, with a sloping floor underneath, and two drains in which to catch liquid runoff from the table. Both families were convinced it was used for embalming.

Still, taking into account that it very well could've been a funeral home at one time you have to figure that when you have a place that sees so many souls passing through it, you're bound to get the good along with the bad. And, as the world goes, the hunger of the darkness is insatiable. Positive energy dissipates quickly without having a willing conduit but negative energy will grow claws and dig in, unwilling to let go. There may have been a few lost souls hanging onto the place, trapped inside the walls of the last place their earthly bodies knew.

During my research I continued to hear additional stories about the satanic rituals that allegedly took place there but I give these little stock. This *was* the late eighties, after all, and a time when the great devil worshipping scare of Eastern Kentucky was going on. (A very fascinating phenomena that I write more in-depth about in my book *Haunted Estill County*. What it basically comes down to is that most empty buildings at that time were rampant with rumors regarding satanic rituals and those involved with the counterculture movement were often dubbed as "Satanist," usually based on nothing more than their clothing and music styles.)

Still, if the house was indeed empty for long periods of time then I have no doubt teenagers and random mischief makers hung out there. That's just what happens. Maybe some partied, and maybe some really *did* bring in Ouija boards and candles. But I take the satanic rituals story with a small grain of salt.

The Native American history of the general region is true, however, and well-documented. The state has now even placed historic markers in several parts of that end of the county to denote the Native American settlement and history.

According to my research, the area was home to the largest, and perhaps even the *only*, permanent Native American settlement. The village's original name is even what gives us our state name. Daniel Boone was once captured and kept prisoner there. It's suspected that thousands of Native Americans lived in the vicinity off and on for years. They hunted, traded, and made their homes there. It was a beautiful, fertile valley and had plentiful resources. The village covered more than three-thousand acres. Everyone wanted it, including the settlers. The settlement was eventually burnt to the ground and the only proof that it was ever there are a few of the burial mounts that haven't been disturbed. Unfortunately, many *were* disturbed over the years.

Not only did the inhabitants die of natural causes, but settlers talked of seeing a fire pit with a locust pole, a place where occupants were burned after committing dire crimes. And then, of course, there were the killings committed by the settlers themselves.

Are there some unsettled natives roaming the lands long after their deaths? Perhaps. A farm house (not Laura's former house but another one not too far away) was built on top of one particular burial mound. The bones were disturbed and discarded as the walls went up. This was, of course, back before we attempted to preserve the burial mounds for what they are and took more care with the Native remains. This particular spot is on record for the remains that were uncovered. It's highly possible that there are others out there underneath structures that we aren't aware of.

I've continued to conduct research on the valley and frequently cruise the internet seeking stories from those who might be familiar with the house. Nothing has ever come up. I hope that in a future update I'll be able to talk more with Dena's family and gather more experiences regarding their time in the home.

Author's Note

Although the preceding story is true, it goes without saying that I wasn't there inside the house at the time of the events. I am going on the words of ten witnesses. I have no reason to doubt them. There are many aspects of the story that I can verify myself. The house *did* have a peculiar vibe to it. My mother and I still talk about how unsettled we felt during our brief time there.

When I think about the house I always remember the darkness and suffocating feel of the interior. Even in broad daylight the kitchen and living room were gloomy and uninviting despite the family's efforts to decorate and illuminate it. I vividly recall the stench that arose from the window leading to the cellar, as well as the table positioned in the middle of the room. I also remember the way Laura shook all the way back to our house, the controlled fear I heard in Jimmy's voice when he called us to come and get her, the way their voices shook when they relayed the events to us afterwards, and the physical appearance of the children when we took Laura home the first time.

For many different reasons I have changed the names of those involved in this story. The children are all grown now and all have children of their own yet they continue to live in the same area. It's not a large place and they would be easily identifiable if their true names were given. For their own privacy I felt it necessary to keep their true identities to myself, although if any of them want to step forward in the future and talk about their experiences that would be fine.

    I continue to be friends with all the girls. In fact, when I was a teenager I became closer to Brenda than almost anyone else. With Laura having a steady boyfriend and working long hours, Brenda started visiting me regularly. She and Laura have been the closest things I have had to sisters and I couldn't love them more if we were blood. Brenda and Laura continued to stay with me over the years, go on family vacations with us, and support me. Laura was my maid of honor at my wedding; Brenda was a bridesmaid. Laura planned my first son's baby shower and, at the age of twenty-six, was there with my husband, holding my other hand as I gave birth.

Visit Amazon

Did you enjoy reading *Two Weeks*? A review on Amazon is like leaving an author a tip! Every little bit helps and no review is too short! If you liked what you just read, please take a moment to write a few words on Amazon at:

http://www.amazon.com/Two-Weeks-True-Haunting-Hauntings-ebook/dp/B013USPH1A/

About the author:

Rebecca Patrick-Howard is the author of several books including a true haunting series and a paranormal mystery series about a woman who sees the past through her camera. She lives in eastern Kentucky with her husband and two children.

Other Books

Visit Rebecca's Amazon author page for links to more books! http://www.amazon.com/Rebecca-Patrick-Howard/e/B00DYWEETE/

Rebecca's other books include:

Taryn's Camera Series

Windwood Farm (Book 1)

Griffith Tavern (Book 2)

Dark Hollow Road (Book 3)

Shaker Town (Book 4)

Jekyll Island (Book 5)

True Hauntings

Four Months of Terror

A Summer of Fear

The Maple House

Two Weeks

Three True Tales of Terror

Haunted Estill County

More Tales from Haunted Estill County

Other Books

Coping with Grief: The Anti-Guide to Infant Loss

Three Minus Zero

Estill County in Photos

Finding Henry: A Journey Into Eastern Europe

Haunted: Ghost Children A Collection of Stories from Beyond

Visit her website at www.rebeccaphoward.net to sign up for her newsletter to receive free books, special offers, and news.

Windwood Farm *excerpt*

After several hours of what she thought was pretty good work on her part, Taryn stepped back and admired her own work, gave herself a pat on the back, and took a break. "Well done, old girl," she said aloud and then *literally* gave herself a pat on the back because, after all, she believed if you didn't do it, then nobody else would.

The sun had come out by then and the ground was starting to dry, but it was still very muddy so she headed to the car and sat on the hood while she ate her lunch—leftover Subway from the night before.

Reagan had taken the boards off the windows like she had asked, and now that the sun had risen in the sky it caught the upstairs window and the glare made it appear to wink at her. In fact, it seemed to look right at her. Shielding her eyes, she turned away. "Damn it," she muttered, as she looked at the ground and took another bite. The glare was so bright, however; she couldn't ignore it.

She had grown used to the uneasy feeling she'd developed on the first day and thought she might be making friends with the house. It didn't feel as unwelcoming to her as it did in the beginning and she was almost certain it had even preened a little today while she was painting it, as though it knew it was posing for something that would make it immortal.

Taryn was not a religious person, and wasn't even sure she believed in God, or one powerful entity at all, but she did believe in energy and nature and if there was something bigger than herself in the universe, she always felt it outside when she was alone. She never found it inside the walls of a church or listening to someone preach. Sometimes, while she was painting, she'd get so lost in thought and deep into her picture that she even thought she might becoming a part of it, or with the world around her. It was the closest thing she'd ever had to a religious experience and the feeling of euphoria it gave her was similar to the one she'd gotten off some pain pills when she'd had her wisdom teeth removed.

All of a sudden, a loud crash from inside the house sang out and caused her to jump off the hood and drop her sandwich to the ground. "So much for the five-second rule," she cursed as she watched it immediately get covered with mud and ants. She was hungry, but not *that* hungry.

Still, she was curious about the noise. She didn't think anyone was in the house and it had been a couple of days since she'd been inside. "Eh, why not?" she mumbled, and made her way to the front door. "What's it going to do?"

Always taken a little aback by the amount of darkness that existed even with the windows uncovered, it took her a moment to adjust her eyes when she stepped inside. The living room was cleared of any items and was stark and empty. Taryn thought this made it feel less intimidating than before, as though the boxes had made it feel more lived in, as though someone was coming back. Even the curtains were gone. The peeling wallpaper was still on the walls, though, and it gently flapped as she walked by, stirred by her movements, the only testament to the fact she was actually there.

The hardwood floors were still rock-solid, despite Reagan's concerns, and didn't make a sound as she moved through the rooms. Not a squeak was made. She was surprised by the lack of dust and smiled at the fact that Mrs. Jones had dusted them; that effort was made to sweep the house before it was demolished. It must be a southern thing to clean something before killing it; to fix something before destroying it. She marveled at the beautiful fireplace mantle, so detailed and ornate and yet at the staircase banister, so simple and plain. There seemed to be no rhyme or reason as to why money was spent on some fixtures and not on others. Clearly, the original owners had possessed money, yet had been selective about how it was spent.

The dining room and kitchen were also bare of belongings, as were the downstairs closets. There obviously wasn't anything on the downstairs level that could have made such a loud noise that she would have heard it from the outside. At any rate, it was as quiet as a church now, or a library. It was hard to imagine this place ever filled with the sounds of a family: laughter, singing, dancing, chattering...Yet the house must have possessed such things and been host to such activities at one time, right? Someone lived in the house and loved it once. Yet there were no echoes of this former life in it now. She could barely even hear her own breathing.

Without the boards on the windows and door, it was easier to see. She thought (hoped) the extra light might make the house feel more gracious, yet the welcoming feeling she'd experienced outside disappeared as soon as she stepped through the front door.

Once she circled through the downstairs, she made her way to the first set of stairs in the living room and put her foot on the first step. All at once, a roar so loud, she felt as though her ear drums would pop from the deafening sound filled the room to a raucous level. Staggering, she fell backward and scraped her lower back against the wooden stairs behind her. As she clutched at her chest, she pushed against an invisible force that seemed to thrust against her. The rumble continued all around her, filling the air at an incredible volume, the sound neither man nor animal.

An astonishing wind swept through the room and up the staircase, whipping her hair around her and sending hot air down her throat, making her unable to talk or scream. Gasping for breath, she struggled to talk or breathe and began choking, gagging, wheezing. The front door, which she'd left open, closed with a bang. In horror, she watched small cracks appear in the living room windows and then watched as the glass shattered and flew out into the yard in hundreds of pieces. Using her hands and sheer strength, Taryn managed to grab onto the banister and pull her way up, inch by inch. Finally, by wrapping her legs around the banister, straddling it, and turning her back to the door and wind, she caught her breath. Using what breath she had left, she screamed with everything she had, "WHAT DO YOU WANT!?"

As quickly as it started, everything stopped.

Taryn was left on the banister, like a little kid who had simply been caught sliding down from the top of the stairs. There was utter stillness again with no sign that anything had happened, other than the fact that the windows were broken and the door was closed.

Shaken, she unwound herself from the banister and ran out the front door, not bothering to close it behind her. She'd let the ghost deal with that.

Available on Amazon!

Download all 4 books in the Taryn's Camera series in one bundle and save 30% off the individual prices! (Or, read them for FREE with Kindle Unlimited!)

http://www.amazon.com/Taryns-Camera-Book-Collection-Paranormal-ebook/dp/B014AQ7EZ8/

Two Weeks

Copyright © 2015 by Rebecca Patrick-Howard

www.rebeccaphoward.net

Published by Mistletoe Press

All rights reserved. No part of this book may be reproduced, scanned, or distributed in any printed or electronic form without permission.

First Edition: September 2015

Printed in the United States of America

Made in the USA
Las Vegas, NV
05 May 2023